Taylor Icon of our times
her life. her music. her style.

Carolyn McHugh

sona
BOOKS

sona BOOKS

© Danann Media Publishing Limited 2024

First published in the UK 2024 by Sona Books an imprint of Danann Media Publishing Ltd.

WARNING: For private domestic use only, any unauthorised copying, hiring, lending or public performance of this book is illegal.

CAT NO: SON0609

Photography courtesy of

Getty images:

Kevin Mazur	Jun Sato/GC Images	Foundation	Tony R. Phipps
Dave Hoga	Ethan Miller	Angela Weiss/AFP	Nicholas Kamm
Rob Verhorst/Redferns	Jeff Kravitz/FilmMagic	Raymond Hall/GC	Neilson Barnard
Sandra Mu	Michael Buckner	Mark Metcalfe/TAS	Peter Nicholls
Christopher Polk/Billboards2012	Emma McIntyre/AMA2019	Andreas Rentz	Brendon Thorne/Stringer
Christopher Polk/TAS	Rick Diamond/WireImage	AFP/Stringer	Rick Diamond
Kevork Djansezian	TAS Rights Management 2020	Sean Zanni	Larry Busacca/TAS
Dimitrios Kambouris/LP5	Rich Fury	TAS Rights Management 2021	Antonin Utz
Sascha Schuermann	Robert Gauthier/Los Angeles Times	JMEnternational	Peter Parks
John Medina	Taylor Hill/FilmMagic	Amy Sussman	Charley Gallay/Stringer
Kevin Winter	John Shearer/AMA2019	Kevin Mazur/TAS	Variety
John Medina	Attitude Magazine	Axelle/Bauer-Griffin	Theo Stroomer / Stringer
Valerie Macon/AFP	Alliance for Women in Media	Robyn Beck	

Other images Alamy, Wiki Commons

Cover design Audrey Alexander
Book design Darren Grice at Ctrl-d
Layout design Alex Young at Cre8ive
Proof reader Cameron thurlow
Editor Mathilde Pineau-Valencienne

All rights reserved. No Part of this title may be reproduced or transmitted in any material form (including photocopying or storing it in any medium by electronic means and whether or not transiently or incidentally to some other use of this publication) without the written permission of the copyright owner, except in accordance with the provisions of the Copyright, Designs and Patents Act 1988. Applications for the copyright owner's written permission should be addressed to the publisher.

This is an independent publication and it is unofficial and unauthorised and as such has no connection with Taylor Swift or her management or any other organisation connected in any way whatsoever with the artist or artists featured in the book.

Printed in Malaysia.
ISBN: 978-1-915343-83-3

Contents

Taylor: **Introduction** 8

Taylor: **Person of the year** 16

Taylor: **Her art** 50

Taylor: **Her brand** 82

Taylor: **Her fans** 110

Taylor: **Her values** 140

Taylor:
Writer and hero of her own story

Introduction

Taylor Swift is the reigning queen of the global music scene, a cultural phenomenon whose influence extends far beyond catchy tunes and chart-topping albums. With her exceptional talent, shrewd business acumen, and unwavering courage, she's become an emblem of resilience, empowerment, and innovation - redefining what it means to be a modern-day icon. She is undeniably the biggest pop star on the planet and arguably the most famous woman in the world.

Since arriving on the country music scene in 2006 as a teenage sensation who captivated audiences with her heartfelt lyrics and infectious melodies, she has had a meteoric rise to fame – on her terms.

Supremely talented, smart and brave, she is the writer and hero of her own story, she's become much more than a mainstream chart-topping artist – she's a powerhouse entrepreneur, a dedicated philanthropist, and a fearless advocate for change.

Taylor has reinvented herself with each album release, highlighting her versatility as an artist and cementing her status as a musical chameleon. Her songs have tackled issues of love, heartbreak, and self-discovery, their lyrics resonating with fans around the world. But it is her unwavering commitment to authenticity and vulnerability that sets her apart. In an industry often plagued by artifice, Taylor remains refreshingly genuine, unafraid to share her triumphs and tribulations with the world.

Taylor: Introduction

Taylor Swift arrives at the 41st Annual Academy Of Country Music Awards held at the MGM Grand Garden Arena on May 23, 2006 in Las Vegas

She is settled among that rarified group of artists, including Elvis Presley and Madonna, capable of combining critical acclaim with commercial success. Her impact on the music industry is unparalleled. With a string of record-breaking albums and an impressive collection of Grammy Awards (14 and counting), she's proven time and again that she's not just here to make music – she's here to make history.

When her re-recording of her *1989* album (*1989 Taylor's Version*), celebrated its fifth week at #1 on the Billboard 200 chart in late 2023, Taylor beat Elvis Presley's record for the most weeks atop the chart by a solo artist. With her industry market share for the year coming in at an impressive 1.72%, it means that if Taylor were her own musical genre, she'd rank ninth for 2023, which is bigger than jazz. Talk about dominating the charts.

Taylor: Introduction

From her groundbreaking achievement as the only artist to win the Grammy for Album of the Year four times, to her unprecedented financial success as the first musician to become a billionaire solely through music, Taylor's legacy is one for the ages.

In addition to her Grammy wins, Taylor's trophy cabinet is overflowing with accolades. She holds the record for the most awards at both the American Music Awards and the Billboard Music Awards, and she has been included on prestigious lists like Time 100 and Forbes Celebrity 100 multiple times.

And her influence now extends far beyond the realm of music. Taylor is a savvy entrepreneur and philanthropist, a trailblazer and role model. She has leveraged her platform to champion causes close to her heart, from women's and gay rights to musicians' remuneration. Her influence is now so great that Time magazine selected her as its Person of the Year 2023.

Taylor during her 2012 Speak Now World Tour

Taylor Swift attends the 65th Grammy Awards

But Taylor's real USP is her unwavering connection with her fans, the Swifties. From intimate acoustic performances to larger-than-life stadium tours, she's forged a bond with her audience that transcends mere fandom – it's a shared journey of growth. Swifties aren't just listeners; they're co-conspirators, and confidants, united by a common love for music and a shared belief in the power of storytelling.

Swifties have gathered in such numbers during Taylor's huge and wildly successful 2023/24 Eras world tour – a record-breaking series of shows – as to make it officially the highest-grossing music tour of all time. It features songs from her 11 hit albums including US#1 hits including *We Are Never Ever Getting Back Together, Shake It Off, Blank Space, Bad Blood, Look What You Made Me Do, Cardigan, Willow, All Too Well, Anti-Hero, Cruel Summer* and varying tracks from her latest album *The Tortured Poets Department*.

Eras has not only broken every attendance and revenue record going, but also boosted the economies of the countries and cities where it has played. It has made Taylor herself a billionaire.

As she continues to shatter records and redefine the music industry, Taylor Swift remains an indefatigable force, a beacon of inspiration for generations to come. And as this book explores her unparalleled journey to superstardom, one thing becomes abundantly clear: there's no stopping Taylor Swift.

Taylor's trophies

14 **Grammy awards** (including a record four for Album of the Year)
40 **American Music Awards** (a record)
40 **Billboard Music Awards** (a record)
4 **Video of the Year wins at the MTV Video Music Awards** (a record)
3 **Global Recording Artist** of the Year titles from the International Federation of the Phonographic Industry.
3 **inclusions on the prestigious Time 100 list** (2009, 2015, 2019).
118 **Guinness World Records** (as of Dec 2023) including being the most streamed act on Spotify in 2023 with more than 26.1 billion streams worldwide.
36.6 **billion streams** (all platforms combined) – a figure undoubtedly boosted by her record-breaking 2023/24 Eras tour.

The opening night of the Eras Tour at State Farm Stadium on March 17, 2023 in Glendale, Arizona

Taylor won five awards including Favourite Pop Album award for 'Red (Taylor's Version) at the 2022 American Music Awards

Taylor:

Taylor: Icon of our times

Person of the year

Breaking records is par for the course for Taylor Swift, but even she must have had pause for thought when *Time* magazine chose her as its 'Person of the Year' 2023, making her the first musician ever to gain that distinction.

The title is awarded for having had the most influence on global events over the past year. Consider that previous recipients have included world leaders and business visionaries, along with, most recently, Greta Thunberg and Volodymyr Zelensky, and you get some idea of the impact Taylor Swift has made during her 18 years of stardom.

'While her popularity has grown across the decades, 2023 is the year that Swift, 33, achieved a kind of nuclear fusion: shooting art and commerce together to release an energy of historic force,' the editorial said. *Time's* editor-in-chief Sam Jacobs went on to describe Taylor Swift as 'the rare person who is both the writer and hero of her own story', adding that she had 'found a way to transcend borders and be a source of light'.

The *Time* award came as Taylor was midway through her glorious, sell-out, record-breaking, retrospective Eras concert tour. Each show is a sweeping arc covering her entire career so far – her artistic 'eras'. Taylor performs 44+ songs, celebrating her 17-year, 10-album trajectory, in an epic show that runs well over three hours and has set the standard for bedazzling performance and state of the art production for years to come.

Demand for the sellout tour was so fierce that websites crashed as fans clamoured for a seat. It's the first music tour to gross over a billion dollars. Concert industry experts *Pollstar* predict that the tour will gross US$1.4bn (£1.1bn) making it the highest earning tour by any artist, anywhere in the world – ever – and beating the previous record set by Sir Elton John with his mammoth farewell tour. The 'Taylor Swift' effect when her show hits town has boosted the economies of all the cities and countries in which she played. The effect was so startling that politicians from Thailand, Hungary, and Chile urged her to come and play in their countries. It's a phenomenon that's come to be known as 'Swiftonomics'.

Taylor: Person of the year

Taylor Swift for the 81st annual Golden Globe Awards at the Beverly Hilton in Beverly Hills, California on Sunday, January 7, 2024

Critically acclaimed, the sell-out tour received five star ratings and rave reviews, described variously as 'a three-hour, career-spanning victory lap', (*Rolling Stone*) 'one of the most ambitious, spectacular, and charming stadium pop shows ever seen' (*Daily Telegraph*) and a 'masterclass' (*LA Times*).

There was also high praise for Taylor's energetic and whole-hearted performance. She never flags, despite the demands placed on her by the show's length and intensity, plus the complications of it being divided into 10 segments, each one a concept devoted to an album, or era. The only album without its own 'world' and set list is her eponymous debut, although on her opening night Taylor included that album's hit single *Tim McGraw* as one of the 'surprise songs' during the acoustic section of the performance, which varies every show.

Taylor: Person of the year

Taylor Swift performs "The Man" during the first of her three sold-out Tampa shows on the Eras tour, at Raymond James Stadium, Thursday, April 13, 2023

Poster for Sam Wrench's documentary about the Eras Tour concert performed by the one and only Taylor Swift

Having first found fame as a 16-year-old country singer in 2006, with her self-titled album *Taylor Swift*, she has provided the soundtrack to the lives of young women the world over. She made country music cool, consolidating her debut with the follow up *Fearless* in November 2008. This was a triumph – making Taylor the youngest artist in history to have the Billboard best-selling album of the year in 2009. It was also critically acclaimed as 2009's album of the year by both the Country Music Association and the Academy of Country Music.

Taylor Swift performs in Kansas City on May 11, 2007

Then came the 2010 Grammy awards, where *Fearless* won four of the prizes, including the hotly contested prize for album of the year – one of the most prestigious awards in the music industry. By the time of the ceremony in January 2010, Taylor had just turned 20 and was the youngest person ever to have won the award.

Taylor: Person of the year

With worldwide sales topping 12 million, *Fearless* remains among the biggest selling albums of the 21st century so far and a standout in Taylor's discography.

With its honest lyrics, catchy melodies, and signature storytelling of love and heartbreak, the album proved to be her coming of age masterpiece, confirming her arrival on the country-pop music scene as its new princess. Unlike the country stars of old, who had attracted largely middle-aged audiences, Taylor was attracting a new, much younger demographic.

On top of that, it bridged the gap between country and mainstream pop music so that Taylor was able to straddle both worlds. She was to continue hopping between the two charts for several years, and albums.

Having toured for years supporting other artists, Taylor now had enough clout to headline her own show and the Fearless Tour, which ran from April 2009 to July 2010, attracted a total audience of 1.2 million people and grossed $66.5 million.

There was a real youthful exuberance about her performance. Now operating on a world stage, Taylor had rubber-stamped her claim to be the next big thing in popular music.

Despite this precocious success, and never one to sit back on her laurels, Taylor had begun working on her third album *Speak Now* almost as soon as *Fearless* had been released.

Taylor Swift at the Grammy Awards, 2010

Taylor: Icon of our times

Speak Now marked a critical point in Taylor's career by documenting her transition from adolescent to adult star, now ready to speak her truth having, for the first time, written every track by herself. Released just two months before her 21st birthday, the album illustrated how Taylor now had completely different inspiration and experience of real, rather than imagined, love and heartbreak. While it was also the first collection of songs she had written as a 'star', rather than a largely unknown American teenager, she had still managed to tap into the themes which resonated with her audiences, such as, on this album, simply the process of 'growing up'.

Taylor: Person of the year

Taylor Swift performs on the opening night of her Speak Now tour at the LG Arena on March 23, 2011 in Birmingham, England

Following its release in October 2010 the album sold an impressive 1,047,000 copies in its first week, almost doubling the opening week sales of *Fearless*. Notably, *Speak Now* became the first album in over two years to pass the million-copy milestone in its debut week. There was a second massively successful tour, promoting the album, which ran from February 2011 to March 2012. Critics praised everything from its sheer visual impact to Taylor's performance and connection with the audience. It became the highest-grossing female and solo tour of 2011, earning Taylor over $40 million.

The stage was set for Taylor to begin her transition to the mainstream pop charts. This she did with her fourth album *Red* in 2012 - the album which boldly fulfilled Taylor's wish to move from country star to major league player and one of the most successful artists in the world.

The final bow at Taylor Swift's 111th show on her Speak Now World Tour at Vector Arena on March 18, 2012 in Auckland, New Zealand

Taylor: Person of the year

The pop hooks in tracks such as *I Knew You Were Trouble* and *We Are Never Ever Getting Back Together* were phenomenal, while the lyrics were generally among the most insightful she had ever produced.

Keen to find a new sound to expand her musical appeal, Taylor and her team brought in two Swedish producers, Max Martin, and Shellback, for her fourth album *Red*. Martin and Shellback were proven hit makers who were shaking up the mainstream charts, and who had a starry back catalogue, including work with Britney Spears and Ariana Grande. While her record company Big Machine still promoted the album's country credentials, and the track list included some country ballads, the most successful tracks were undeniably pure pop. Critics noted Taylor's vocals had lost their country twang.

Beyond the tracks: The legacy of Red

Red sold 1.2 million copies during its first week on sale in the US - more than any album in a single week since 2002.

By the following year it had achieved **worldwide sales of six million**.

The album spent **seven weeks at the top of the US Billboard 200 album chart**, giving Taylor the accolade of being the first female artist and only the second act since The Beatles to have three consecutive albums at number one for at least six weeks.

It was **Taylor's first #1 album in the UK**, while also topping the charts in Australia, Canada, and New Zealand.

Red earned over 50 accolades, including four nominations at the 56th Annual Grammy Awards.

The single *I Knew You Were Trouble* won **Best Female Video** at the 2013 MTV Video Music Awards.

Taylor herself won **Best Female Country Artist** at the 2012 American Music Awards and **Artist of the Year** at the 2013 ceremony. She also received the Nashville Songwriters Association's 'Songwriter/Artist Award' for the sixth consecutive year in 2013.

Taylor Swift accepts the Woman of the Year award onstage at the 2012 Billboard Music Awards

Taylor: Person of the year

Taylor then returned to the road with the colossal Red Tour which ran from March 2013 to June 2014, becoming the most successful tour by a country artist of all time, grossing $150 million. It was a massive production, dramatic and super-slick, featuring 15 dancers, four backing singers, a seven-piece band, multi-level stages, hydraulics, confetti showers and costume changes galore.

Praised for its elaborate stage production, energy, and guest appearances by various artists, the Red Tour solidified Taylor's status as one of the top touring acts in the music industry.

Now recognised and respected as a musician, Taylor was named Woman of the Year by Billboard in 2012 – making her the youngest artist to receive that honour – listed by Forbes as the highest earning star aged under 30 and included among Billboard's Top 40 Money Makers in Music.

In autumn 2013 the Country Music Association presented Taylor with its highest honour, the Pinnacle Award, which is only given occasionally and hadn't been presented since 2005. It was created 'to honour an artist who has achieved both national and international prominence through concert performances and record sales at levels unique in country music'.

At the age of just 23, having picked up the biggest prize in country music, and achieved global fame in the process, Taylor really had nothing left to prove as a country artist. So she decided to reinvent herself completely as a mainstream pop star.

The result was her fifth album, 2014's landmark and blockbusting *1989,* which saw Taylor smash through into the mainstream as a fully packaged international pop phenomenon. Titled after the year of her birth, *1989* was quite simply a euphoric pop masterpiece which won her a second Grammy for Album of the Year.

Its synth-pop tracks – including a clutch of chart-topping singles including *Blank Space, Shake it Off* and *I Knew You Were Trouble* - ensured Taylor shed her country image once and for all and transitioned to pure pop star. She worked with co-writers and producers including Jack Antonoff for the first time and with Max Martin and Shellback again.

Taylor Swift performs at the 54th Annual Grammy Awards

Taylor: Person of the year

The album's content was a very positive riposte to the criticisms she had begun receiving about her personal life and relationship issues and included some of her best songs to date. Critics praised her for bringing emotional engagement into mainstream pop.

Beyond the tracks: The legacy of *1989*

Topping the Billboard 200 chart for 11 weeks, *1989* became **Taylor's fourth American #1 album** and her third consecutive album to sell above one million copies in its first week – a new record for any artist.

With sales of 1.29 million in its first week, *1989* had the biggest seven-day sales of any release since 2002, according to Nielsen SoundScan.

It won Album of the Year at the 2016 Grammys, making Taylor the first female artist ever to win the prize twice. The album also picked up the **Grammy for Best Pop Vocal Album** and appeared on several 2010s best albums lists. *Rolling Stone* went on to feature it in their 2020 revised list of the 500 Greatest Albums of All Time.

The album also made clear that **Taylor had shed her country roots completely**; there was no marketing push in the country music media at all. In fact in several interviews to promote the album Taylor mentioned the idea of a 'rebirth'.

Taylor Swift performs onstage during The 1989 World Tour on June 13, 2015 at Lincoln Financial Field in Philadelphia, Pennsylvania

Taylor: Person of the year

Her 'The 1989 World Tour' ran from May to December 2015, spanning multiple legs across Asia, North America, Europe, and Oceania and setting new records for concert attendance and revenue. It grossed over $250 million in ticket sales worldwide, making it one of the highest-grossing concert tours of that year and then the entire decade, bringing in over US$199.4 million in North America alone, smashing the previous all-time high of $162 million set by the Rolling Stones 10 years before.

During its record-breaking run of 85 shows, Taylor played to over 2.2 million fans in total, making it the best attended tour of all time.

As always, Taylor was closely involved with the planning and design of her tour which was seven months in conception and three months in rehearsal. It was a challenge for Taylor and her team to create the intimate experience she wanted for her fans, while needing to perform in huge stadiums to accommodate them. Production-wise, the tour featured elaborate stage design, intricate choreography, and state-of-the-art visual effects, creating an immersive experience for audiences. Taylor's own performances were praised for their energy, charisma, and connection with fans.

The set was predominantly of songs from *1989*, but she also included songs from her back catalogue. Many of the shows featured special guests including members of her 'squad' of girlfriends, plus other musicians and even sports stars.

After completing the tour Taylor retreated from the spotlight in 2016 - her first break from the music industry in 10 years. Her love life had long attracted unwelcome scrutiny and criticism, so now she had begun a serious relationship with British actor Joe Alwyn she wanted to conduct their romance more privately. So she secretly moved from America to London to be with him and began writing and planning an album which would blow everything out of the water.

The result was *Reputation*, released in November 2017. It was the first new music she had released in three years and to say fans were excited is an understatement. Taylor had gone in a bold and different direction on this, her sixth album, incorporating elements of what was going on elsewhere in music such as rap, hip hop, and R&B. She took inspiration from her tempestuous relationship with the media and the personal difficulties involved in navigating a love life against such a background.

Ditching her innocent and intensely romantic narratives of

old in favour of darker themes around fame, reputation and relationships, Taylor's songs referenced alcohol and sex and included swearing for the first time. She has since described the album as being 'cathartic'.

Produced once again by her long time collaborators Max Martin, Shellback and Jack Antonoff, the album leaned heavily into darker electropop sounds, using synthesisers and manipulated vocals amid other techniques.

The audacious *Look What You Made Me Do* was the first single from that album, accompanied by what is now an iconic video – certainly one of her most creative.

Taylor: Person of the year

The 1989 World Tour Live In Los Angeles at Staples Center on August 22, 2015

Beyond the tracks: The legacy of *Reputation*

Reputation became **Taylor's fourth consecutive album to enter the American charts straight in at #1**, where it remained for four weeks.

First-week sales were over 1.2 million, making Taylor **the first artist to have four consecutive albums sell over a million in the first week of release**. The album also topped the charts in the UK, Canada and Australia.

By the end of 2017 *Reputation* had sold over **4.5 million copies** and become the year's **best-selling album by a female artist**.

Because *Reputation* marked such a significant shift in Taylor's music and public image, it naturally elicited a range of opinions from critics. While many praised her bravery in experimenting with a new edgier persona, some critics found it braggadocious – but why not. Her fans adored it.

In keeping with the anti-media mood of the album, Taylor did not do any press interviews to promote it. Nevertheless it topped the charts for three weeks, becoming her fifth number one hit on US Billboard Hot 100 and also gaining the most plays on Spotify in a single day. *Reputation* also became the top-selling US album of the year.

Taylor Swift accepts Artist of the Year onstage during the 2018 American Music Awards at the Microsoft Theater on October 9, 2018 in Los Angeles

Taylor: Person of the year

By the time her accompanying tour kicked off, Taylor only had her own records to beat – which she did, topping the gross and attendance figures set by the *1989* tour in a series of 53 all-stadium shows which ran from May to November 2018.

The reviews raved about the Reputation shows, which combined Broadway-style theatricality with gothic visuals and costumes, describing the tour as Taylor's best ever. Again she managed to retain a strong connection with her fans despite the huge stage and skyscraper set she commanded.

Taylor Swift performs onstage during the 2018 Reputation Stadium Tour at Soldier Field on June 1, 2018 in Chicago, Illinois

Taylor during the Reputation Stadium Tour

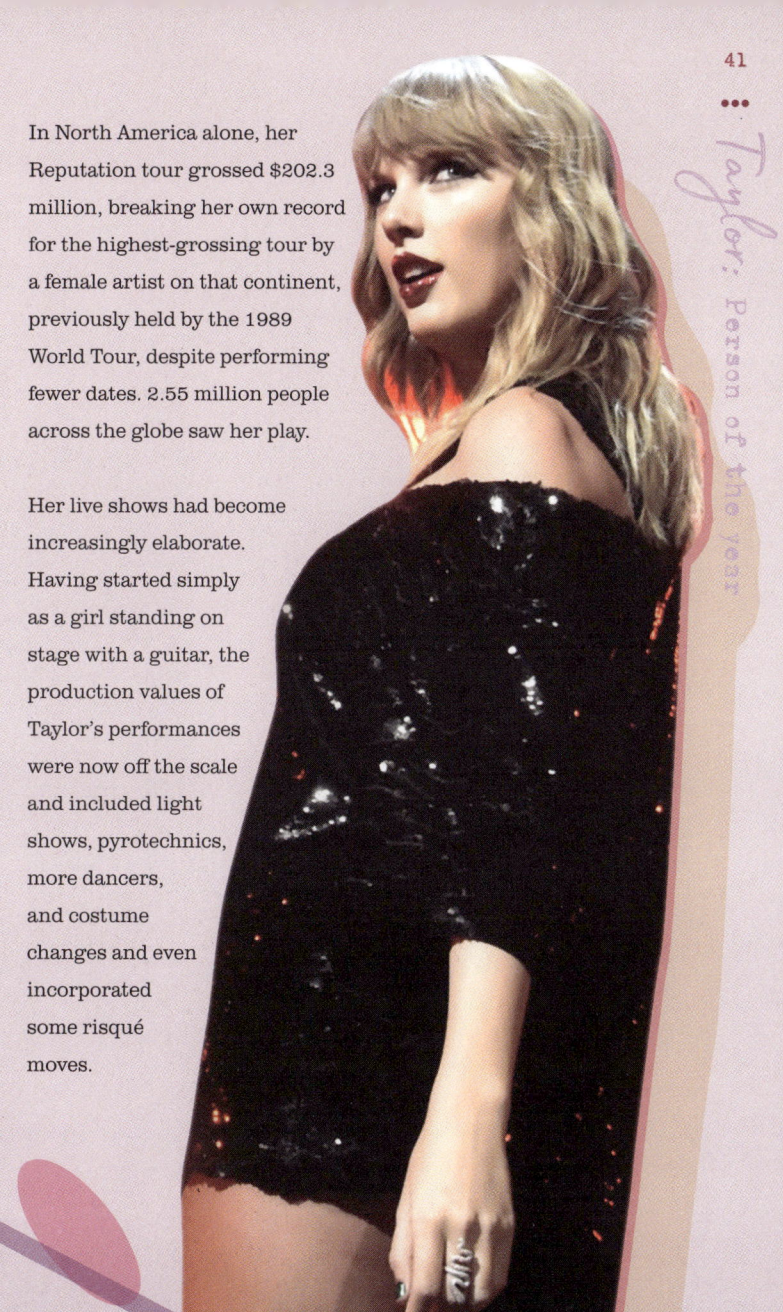

In North America alone, her Reputation tour grossed $202.3 million, breaking her own record for the highest-grossing tour by a female artist on that continent, previously held by the 1989 World Tour, despite performing fewer dates. 2.55 million people across the globe saw her play.

Her live shows had become increasingly elaborate. Having started simply as a girl standing on stage with a guitar, the production values of Taylor's performances were now off the scale and included light shows, pyrotechnics, more dancers, and costume changes and even incorporated some risqué moves.

Taylor: Person of the year

Taylor: Icon of our times

Taylor Swift with president of Big Machine Records Scott Borchetta and Sandy Borchetta

Taylor Swift onstage during the Reputation Stadium Tour at Levi's Stadium on May 11, 2018 in Santa Clara, California

Everything was seamless. Once again she had set the bar stratospherically high.

Following a fall-out with her record company Big Machine, Taylor released her seventh album, 2019's *Lover,* on the Republic label, part of the Universal Music Group.

While it was undoubtedly a multi-million-dollar deal, Taylor made the move as much for her rights as the money because her new contract with UMG agreed that she would own her own masters going forward.

Taylor: Person of the year

Taylor described the upbeat *Lover* album as 'a love letter to love itself', as she looked back over the first 30 years of her life. In the album's liner notes she says that she found a bunch of old diaries which inspired much of her work here.

Containing everything from Nashville twang to electropop influences, the album's release was heralded by two singles, *Me!* and *You Need to Calm Down*, which both reached #2 on the Hot 100 and helped get the album to #1 in the US and around the world. Sales of 3.2 million copies in 2019, made *Lover* the best-selling studio album of the year and gave Taylor the accolade of being the best-selling musician in the world for 2019.

But plans to promote the album any further had to be cancelled because of the worldwide Covid-19 pandemic which put a stop to all festivals and concert tours in 2020, including Taylor's planned sixth tour *Lover Fest*. All the shows, scheduled to begin on 5 April that year, were cancelled as the world closed down.

Having ended 2019 by winning the first ever Billboard Woman of the Decade Award for being 'one of the most accomplished musical artists of all time over the course of the 2010s', Taylor turned her enforced quarantine into an opportunity to build on that achievement throwing herself into a brand new, top secret project – the creation of two new albums, *folklore* and *evermore*.

Taylor: Person of the year

Onstage at the 2019 American Music Awards at the Microsoft Theater, November 24, 2019, Los Angeles, California

Fans were stunned when the surprise albums dropped five months apart in 2020, completely out of the blue. It had only been a year since *Lover* and, given the Covid 19 lockdown as well, no one was expecting any new music. Taylor said that she hadn't really planned it either but had revelled in the unexpected period of uninterrupted creative time and was inspired to write by the many old films and classic books she consumed in the early part of the quarantine. All these fictional narratives encouraged Taylor to give free rein to her own imagination. So, instead of writing about her own life and experiences, she conjured up a host of characters to entertain her fans.

Both albums were fresh and truthful, less showy than much of her previous, more pop-centred, output. Their cottage-core aesthetic, romanticising escaping noisy modern life to return to simpler times, chimed perfectly with the reflective vibe her fans were experiencing during the lockdown.

Her new collaborators on these mesmerising sister albums included Aaron Dessner and his bandmates from US rock band The National, Haim, Marcus Mumford of Mumford & Sons, and Justin Vernon from Bon Iver. The result was an indie, electro-folk, alternative rock offering, driven by guitar and piano, which refreshed the entire 'Taylor Swift' brand.

folklore went on to win the Grammy for Album of the Year in 2021, giving Taylor a record-breaking third win in this category. As well as that the prize meant that she had, quite incredibly, won each of her Grammys with entirely different genres of music; country, pop and now alternative. It also meant she entered the music history books by becoming the first woman, and only the fourth artist ever – to have three wins in that category.

But she wasn't done. Her next album, 2022's *Midnights* - which had amassed a record 184.69 million streams in its first 24 hours of release - also picked up the Grammy for Album of the Year 2024, making Taylor the only artist ever to win that category four times.

The honour capped off a purple patch of post-pandemic creativity and success for Taylor, which one commentator likened to her having entered the 'imperial phase' of her career. Further validation came in January 2024, when Taylor became the first musician ever to top the Billboard Power 100 list, an annual ranking of the most impactful music industry movers and shakers. She even beat Lucian Grainge, CEO of her UMG label.

Taylor: Person of the year

Taylor Swift, winner of Album of the Year for *folklore*, poses in the media room during the 63rd Annual Grammy Awards at Los Angeles Convention Center on March 14, 2021 in Los Angeles, California

How better to celebrate than by doing what she does so well – entertaining her fans. So the Eras Tour – her first in five years - rolled on, taking in over 150 dates between opening in Glendale, Arizona, USA on 17 March 2023 and closing on 8 December 2024 in Vancouver, Canada, filling stadiums across five continents in between.

Every show is divided into 10 sections, each one devoted to an album with a conceptual re-creation of the aesthetic, feel and fashion of its 'era'. So think fringing for *Fearless*, snakes for *Reputation*, pastels for *Lover*, dark cape for *evermore* and you get the idea – everything sparkling with crystals of course.

The staging is simply phenomenal and works for the huge power numbers as well as the more intimate sections. There's a main stage, a diamond stage, and a gigantic catwalk stretching out nearly the entire length of the stadium and a hydraulic platform which rises and falls to create different performance areas.

The sets aim to create a 'world' for each era and include incredible structures and special effects such as a mossy cabin for *folklore*, trees for *evermore* and a dolls house-type home for *Lover*.

But even accounting for the state-of-the-art technical wizardry, the most amazing aspect of the whole show is Taylor herself. She is simply a powerhouse, commanding the stage as she sings and dances in stunning performances of her songs, pitch perfect and on point as she manages 16 costume changes and props galore, all the while coping with large-scale, high-tech set swaps and executing theatrical stunts worthy of a Broadway show.

The rapturous nightly audiences are averagely 70,000 strong, but some stadiums have accommodated over 95,000 people. They certainly get their money's worth as the show, like the whole Taylor Swift phenomenon, is simply in a league of its own.

Taylor: Person of the year

Performing at the 63rd Annual Grammy Awards broadcast on March 14, 2021

Taylor:

Taylor: Icon of our times

Her art

Taylor's artistic evolution is truly unique.

To paint an accurate portrait of her art you have to begin with her music which has made an indelible mark on the musical landscape, not just with catchy melodies and poignant lyrics, but also through its ability to transcend genres.

Since bursting onto the scene as a country music prodigy, Taylor has redefined the very essence of what it means to be a contemporary artist.

In her early days, when she was armed simply with her guitar and a flair for storytelling, her debut self-titled album introduced the world to her signature blend of heartfelt lyrics and catchy hooks, earning her legions of fans in the country music sphere. With songs like *Teardrops on My Guitar* and *Our Song*, Taylor established herself as a rising star in Nashville, capturing the essence of young love and heartache with an authenticity that resonated deeply with her growing fan base.

However, it was with her transition to pop music that Taylor truly revolutionised the industry. With the release of her album *1989*, she embraced a bold new sound, infusing her music with infectious synth-pop beats and irresistible hooks. Tracks like *Shake It Off* and *Blank Space* showcased her prowess as a pop powerhouse, earning her critical acclaim and commercial success on a global scale.

Her ability to transition seamlessly between genres demonstrated her versatility as an artist and solidified her status as one of the most influential figures in contemporary music. Her journey from country sweetheart to pop sensation is testament to her talent, creativity, versatility and unwavering dedication to her craft.

But her genre-bending prowess doesn't stop there. She continued to push the boundaries of musical conventions with later albums, including *Reputation* and *Lover*, experimenting with different styles and sounds while staying true to her distinctive voice. From the edgy electro-pop of *Look What You Made Me Do* to the dreamy synth-infused melodies of *Cruel Summer*, Taylor consistently defied categorisation, proving that she is a force to be reckoned with in any genre she chooses to explore.

Taylor's family took the brave decision to relocate permanently to Nashville when the buzz around her music grew

At the heart of her art, she's an extraordinary storyteller, willing to mine her personal life and relationships for material, unafraid to bare and share her innermost feelings.

As Taylor put it in an interview with radio station NPR: 'The first thing that I think about when I'm writing my lyrics is directly communicating with the person the song is about. I think what I've learned recently is that it's not heartbreak that inspires my songs, it's not love that inspires my songs; it's individual people that come into my life.'

Throughout her career Taylor has always written about what she knows – never trying to sound or write as older than she is. In that way, and despite her growing fame, she has always shared many of the emotions that other women of her age have experienced. Explaining how she can draw inspiration from anything – a memory or even a glance - Taylor gave the *Washington Post* some further insight as to how she worked, saying 'If you're a good storyteller you can take a dirty look somebody gives you, or if a guy you used to have flirtations with starts dating a new girl, or somebody you're casually talking to says something that makes you so mad – you can create a scenario around that.

Taylor Swift is a master of her art

'For a female to write about her feelings,' she said, 'and then be portrayed as some clingy, insane, desperate girlfriend in need of making you marry her and have kids with her, I think that's taking something that potentially should be celebrated—a woman writing about her feelings in a confessional way—that's taking it and turning it and twisting it into something that is frankly a little sexist. I'm work-crazy. That's the thing that I'm crazy about, that I don't stop thinking about, you know? I think they need to make up these angles because my actual personal life doesn't have a shocking angle to it: I go to work. I come home. I occasionally go out with my friends. I occasionally go on dates.'

Taylor: Her art

More recently, and in a move which further consolidated her success, her 'quarantine' albums *folklore* and *evermore*, along with 2023's *Midnights* have shared entirely fictional narratives.

'...In isolation my imagination has run wild and this album is the result, a collection of songs and stories that flowed like a stream of consciousness. Picking up a pen was my way of escaping into fantasy, history, and memory. I've told these stories to the best of my ability with all the love, wonder, and whimsy they deserve'. Taylor in prologue for *Midnights*

Taylor Swift performs onstage during the Eras Tour

The skilled wordplay and incredible acuity she employs as she captures emotional heights and depth in a single line has even led to academic discussion over her credentials as a writer and poet – throwing up comparisons to such literary titans as Shakespeare, Coleridge, and Wordsworth. The internet is crammed with online quizzes with a chance to choose whether a line is 'Swift or Shakespeare'.

Scholar Sir Jonathan Bate, a former Shakespeare professor at Warwick University, has said he believes Taylor displayed a 'literary sensibility' from her earliest days as a teenager writing her first album.

THE SUNDAY TIME
magazine

In a piece for the *Sunday Times* magazine, headlined, *Why Taylor Swift is a literary giant*, Jonathan Bate analysed how the singer had been inspired by Shakespeare and had succeeded in 'rewriting his darker moments' to make them 'more palatable', including in her song *Love Story*.

Another example is her 2020 track *The Lakes*, a dreamy and poetic ode which featured as a bonus track on the deluxe version of *folklore*. The title is a reference to the British Lake District, which was home to the introspective English romantic poets of the 18th century. Taylor muses about escaping her fame and going there to find peace and protection for herself and her lover.

He also noted instances where Taylor had alluded to or referenced Ernest Hemingway, Robert Frost and Emily Dickinson. The reference to Dickinson was particularly interesting given that Ancestry.com recently revealed that she and Taylor are sixth cousins, three times removed.

Taylor: Icon of our times

Taylor Swift writes lyrics on her arm backstage prior to the first of three sold-out shows at The Prudential Center. The North American portion of The RED Tour

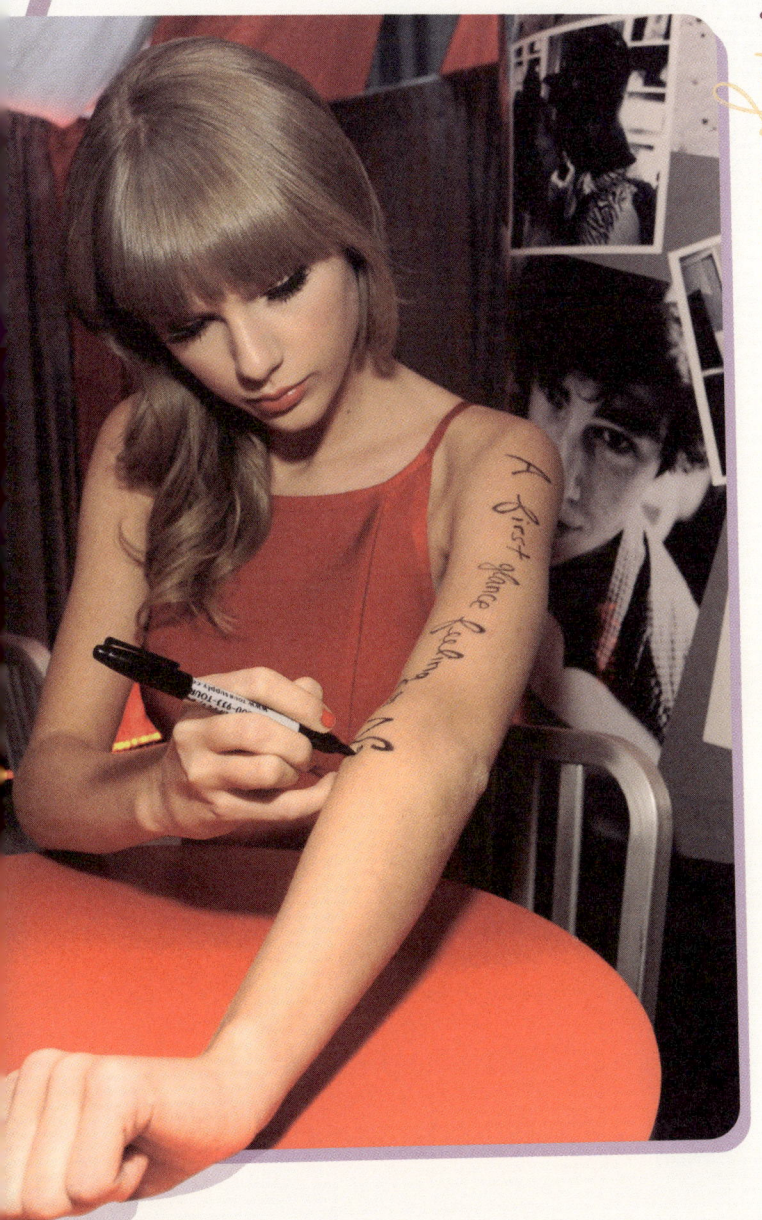

Literary connections

It has been revealed that Taylor is distantly related to the renowned 19th century poet Emily Dickinson. Known for her distinctive style and exploration of profound themes including death, nature and the human psyche, Dickinson wrote nearly 1,800 poems, mainly in the 1850s and 1860s, and is widely credited with revolutionising American poetry.

Her sixth great grandfather, a 17th century English immigrant, was among the early settlers in Connecticut, USA, and, as documented by Ancestry.com, that same man was Taylor's ninth great grandfather, his descendants having married into the Swift family line and settling in Pennsylvania. This makes Emily and Taylor sixth cousins, three times removed.

Taylor has frequently referenced her distant cousin when discussing her inspiration. Speaking at the Nashville Songwriters Association International in 2022, while accepting their award as Songwriter-Artist of the Decade, Taylor said, 'If my lyrics sound like a letter written by Emily Dickinson's great-grandmother while sewing a lace curtain that's me writing in the quill genre'.

Sir Jonathan signed off his piece with the words: 'The enduring advocacy of the distinguished critic Professor Sir Christopher Ricks eventually won Bob Dylan the Nobel Prize in Literature. I'm not sure I would yet go that far for Taylor Swift but watch this space.'

With Taylor's work having single-handedly elevated songwriting to its own art, as distinct from poems, universities and colleges are also now studying her world and work. Renowned educational establishments in the US, including Harvard, University of Texas, New York University, Stanford University and Berklee College of Music, are offering courses and modules on Taylor, covering everything from her lyrics, themes, motifs and literary references to her legacy and societal impact.

The UK's Queen Mary University of London runs a summer school called 'Taylor Swift and Literature' which analyses the literary references, rhymes and word choices in her songs, along with their political, national and historical contexts.

Taylor Swift at the 2023 MTV Video Music Awards

In Belgium, Ghent University has launched a new course dedicated to the literary merit of Taylor's work. Entitled 'Literature: Taylor's Version' it is curated by assistant professor Elly McCausland who writes a regular blog entitled 'Swifterature'. The course takes Taylor's themes, imagery and use of language and uses them to engage with literature 'from the Medieval period to the Victorian' according to the syllabus, including Chaucer's *Troilus and Criseyde*, Shakespeare's *The Tempest* and Charlotte Brontë's *Villette*. More contemporary authors including Margaret Atwood and Simon Armitage also feature.

Taylor Swift poses for a portrait in West Hollywood

'Highly prolific and autobiographical in her songwriting, Swift makes frequent allusions to canonical literary texts in her music', the syllabus continues. 'Using Swift's work as a springboard, we will explore, among other topics, literary feminism, ecocriticism, fan studies, and tropes such as the anti-hero. Swift's enduring popularity stems, at least in part, from the heavily intertextual aspect of her work, and this course will dig deeper to explore its literary roots.'

Dr Swift

In May 2022 Taylor was awarded an honorary doctorate in Fine Arts by New York University.

Using music as the way into a corpus of literature like this is pretty much unheard of. It is certainly all a very long way from where pop music began some 70 years ago. In the early days of rock and roll when the radio airways were thick with meaningless phrases like 'a wop bop a loo bop a lop bam boom' as the opening cry of Little Richard's 1955 hit *Tutti Frutti* and *A Whole Lotta Shakin Going On*, as described by Jerry Lee Lewis in his 1957 rockabilly hit.

But Taylor's influence now goes way beyond her own artistic endeavours. Her success has paved the way for other artists to embrace genre fluidity and artistic experimentation. Her fearless approach to songwriting and production has inspired a new generation of musicians to break free from traditional constraints and forge their own path in the industry. Whether it's blending elements of country, pop, or alternative music, Taylor has shown that creativity knows no bounds, and that true artistry lies in the ability to defy expectations and categorisation.

Yet while Taylor's impact on the music industry cannot be overstated, her artistic influence now transcends the boundaries of music, extending into the realms of fashion, film, and popular culture. She's a trend-setter and fashionista whose appearances on red carpets and in movies have captivated global audiences and bolstered her position as a cultural icon.

As a bona fide fashion icon, known for her impeccable style and trendsetting looks, Taylor turns heads wherever she goes. From glittering gowns on the red carpet to effortlessly chic streetwear, Taylor proves time and again that she's a force to be reckoned with in fashion and continuously dazzles fans with her ever-evolving style.

Many of these fashion choices have become iconic, celebrated for their unique and captivating aesthetics.

Taylor: Her art

One of her standout qualities as a fashionista is her ability to blend classic elegance with modern trends. Whether she's rocking a vintage-inspired ensemble or experimenting with bold prints and colours, Taylor always manages to exude confidence and sophistication. Her fashion choices often reflect her evolving artistic persona, mirroring the themes and narratives of her music.

When it comes to designers, Taylor has a penchant for both established fashion houses and up-and-coming designers alike. She's been spotted wearing creations from iconic brands like Versace and Gucci, showing her affinity for luxury and high fashion. However, Taylor also isn't afraid to champion emerging talent, often choosing to wear pieces from rising stars in the fashion world.

Jack Antonoff and Taylor Swift attend the 65th Grammy Awards 2023 in Los Angeles, California

One of Taylor's favourite designers is undoubtedly Elie Saab, known for his ethereal and romantic designs. Taylor has stunned in Saab's intricate lace gowns and sparkling embellishments, cementing her status as a red carpet darling. She's also a fan of the timeless elegance of Oscar de la Renta, frequently opting for his sleek and sophisticated creations for major events.

Having started out with a country look of cowboy boots and frilly frocks, Taylor has since developed a unique style of her own, undergoing a remarkable transformation with every new album.

As she ventured into the realm of full-fledged pop with her *1989* album, her wardrobe underwent a notable evolution. Embracing a newfound confidence, she began to show more flesh and to wear more vibrant hues, symbolising a departure from her country roots. The transition from country to city chic was marked by the adoption of higher heels and meticulously coordinated outfit sets in a kaleidoscope of colours.

This era in Taylor's fashion journey is truly distinctive, and a real favourite with fans as they witnessed the star embracing a fresh dynamic flair, unlike previous and subsequent eras, where her colour palette appears more restrained.

Away from the promotional whirl, cardigan sweaters have long been a motif, now immortalised in song and reemerging as rural chic in her *folklore* era.

The song *"cardigan"* was one of the lead tracks from the 2020 lockdown *folklore* album and quickly became a fan favourite. The lyrics, which evoke themes of nostalgia, comfort, and longing, resonated deeply with listeners, particularly during a time of global uncertainty and isolation due to the COVID-19 pandemic.

In a stroke of marketing genius, Taylor capitalised on the popularity of the song by releasing a limited edition cardigan inspired by the track's artwork and themes. The cardigan, featuring a cozy knit design adorned with stars, clouds, and other whimsical motifs, quickly sold out and became a coveted fashion item among Swifties and fashion enthusiasts alike.

Beyond its status as a fashion accessory, the cardigan symbolized a sense of connection and solidarity among fans during a challenging period. Many fans shared photos of themselves wearing the cardigan on social media, using the hashtag #cardiganchallenge to declare their love for Taylor and the album.

Taylor Swift wearing an Elie Saab dress at the 47th Annual CMA awards

Fashion Through The Eras:

Taylor Swift's iconic looks Album by Album

Taylor Swift (2006): Sweet and innocent country-inspired outfits, often featuring cowboy boots, sundresses, handkerchief hems and curly hair. ▼

Speak Now (2010): Romantic and whimsical ensembles with vintage flair, including lace dresses and floral patterns. ▼

Fearless (2008): Princess-inspired dresses with glitter, sparkles and frills, reminiscent of fairy tale glamour. ▶

Taylor: Icon of our times

Red (2012):

In the whirlwind of the Red era, Taylor rocked some unforgettable sophisticated yet edgy looks featuring bold red lips, statement accessories, and sleek silhouettes. On stage it was all high-waisted shorts, striped shirts, and a healthy dose of sequins, always stealing the show. ▼

1989 (2014):

Having relocated to New York City, Taylor came to embody that city's 'uptown' vibe. Hanging with her 'squad' of actress and model friends, Taylor rocked retro-inspired, girl-boss outfits with a modern twist, including crop tops and statement jackets. ▼

Reputation (2017):

Dark and edgy ensembles were the vibe for Reputation. Everything had a hint of rockstar glamour, often featuring leather, studs, and dramatic makeup. Serpentine jewellery cast an aura of mystique and power over her look. ▶

Lover (2019):

Colourful and playful looks with a romantic aesthetic, including pastel colours, floral prints, and feminine silhouettes. ▼

evermore (2020):

The *folklore* look evolved, as Taylor enveloped herself in long-sleeved floral maxis and soft woollen coats and sweaters to layer a darker and more mysterious edge over the still cosy but more whimsical designs. ▼

folklore (2020):

Quarantine chic was to the fore here as Taylor unveiled another new look featuring cosy and ethereal outfits with a folk-inspired vibe. Think knitted sweaters, flowy dresses, chunky boots and earthy tones. ▼

Midnights (2022)

On the red carpet, Taylor shone bright in diamonds and sharp suits, flaunting eye-catching textures. At home, she kept it cosy yet chic, rocking cashmere and stripes with effortless style. ▶

Her looks for New York's annual Met Gala are always eagerly anticipated. One of her most iconic fashion moments came at the 2016 Met Gala, where she embraced the event's theme of "Manus x Machina: Fashion in an Age of Technology" with a 'futuristic gladiator' look. She paired a stunning silver Louis Vuitton mini dress with edgy knee-high gladiator sandals for a look which perfectly encapsulated her ability to push boundaries and make a statement with her fashion choices.

To a casual observer, Taylor is well known for her signature 'Reputation - era' style, characterized by edgy, dark ensembles and bold statement pieces. From leather jackets to thigh-high boots, Taylor embraced a more rebellious aesthetic during this period, once again displaying her versatility as a fashion chameleon. Her signature red lip, standing out against her pale skin and blue eyes, led one commentator to describe her as having a red, white, and blue face like the American flag.

A true fashion powerhouse in her own right, with a fearless approach and a penchant for pushing boundaries, Taylor inspires fans and fashionistas alike to embrace their own unique sense of style and self-expression.

This, as well as her strategic collaborations with renowned brands, such as Stella McCartney, has left a bold mark on the entertainment and consumer landscapes.

Swift Style:

Taylor's Most Iconic Red Carpet Moments

2008 MTV Video Music Awards

Hitting the red carpet in a lavender strapless gown adorned with delicate ruching, Taylor's youthful elegance and choice of colour made her stand out. Little did we know that this was just the beginning of Taylor's journey to becoming a trendsetter and superstar.

2009 MTV Video Music Awards

Taylor rocked a shimmering gold KaufmanFranco gown with intricate beading.

2010 Grammy Awards

This sparkling blue KaufmanFranco gown with a plunging neckline and a dramatic open back, showcased her glamorous yet playful style. ▼

2011 Billboard Music Awards

A sleek and modern Elie Saab gown with intricate lace detailing and a daring sheer skirt.

2014 Grammy Awards

A stunning silver Gucci gown with a plunging neckline and crystal-embellished bodice.

2014 Met Gala

Oscar de la Renta again – this time with a dramatic train and intricate floral embroidery, capturing the event's theme of 'Charles James: Beyond Fashion'. ▼

2016 Grammy Awards

Colour-clashing with a vibrant orange Atelier Versace bandeau top and high-waisted, floor-length pink skirt daringly split at the front. ▼

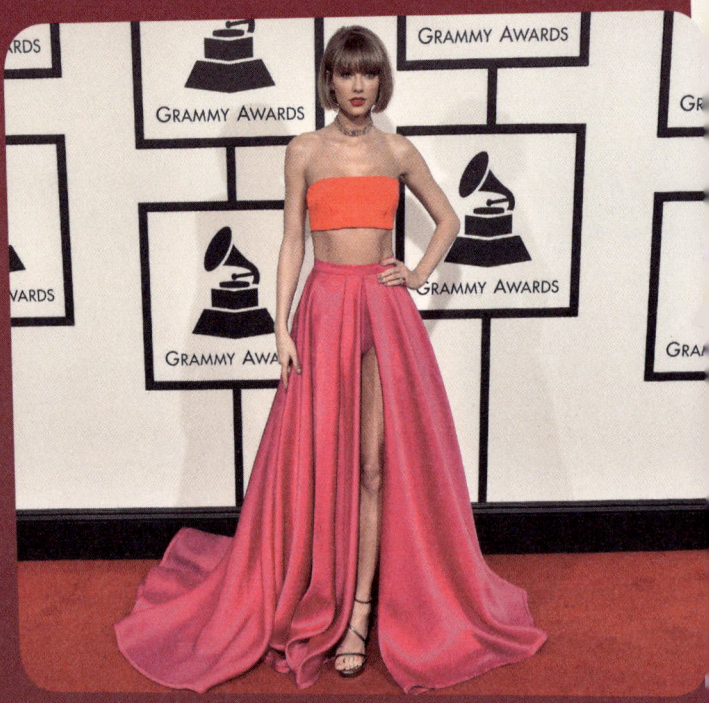

2018 Billboard Music Awards

A soft pink Versace gown with intricate lace detailing and a flowing train.

2019 iHeartRadio Music Awards 2019

A shimmering sequined Rosa Bloom mini playsuit, paired with butterfly heels.

2021 Grammy Awards

An Oscar de la Renta long-sleeved embroidered floral midi dress. ▶

2022 MTV European Music Awards

This David Koma design - a black leotard piece layered underneath a sheer maxi skirt embellished with gemstones - was a nod to the 'naked dress' trend.

2024 Grammy Awards

Glamour personified in a strapless, snow white gown by Schiaparelli accessorised with dramatic black opera-length gloves and a black ribbon choker reminiscent of the *Midnights* clock. ▼

Taylor: Her art

Taylor: Icon of our times

Outside of music and fashion, Taylor has expanded her presence in modern pop culture by appearing on film, both in movies and in her own documentaries. Her acting credits include her appearance in an episode of *CSI Crime Scene Investigation* and guesting on *Saturday Night Live*. She made her movie debut as part of the starry ensemble cast of the 2010 film *Valentine's Day* for which she wrote two original songs. She voiced 'Audrey' in the 2012 animation *The Lorax* and had a small part in 2014's *The Giver*.

In 2019 she played Bombalurina in the musical fantasy film *Cats* – based on the poems of T.S. Eliot. She also worked with the show's composer Andrew Lloyd Webber to co-write the song *Beautiful Ghosts* which features on the soundtrack. 'I was very surprised and very delighted she wanted to have a go at it,' Lloyd Webber told The New York Post. "And I was even more happy it turned out to be such a good lyric. She put a lot of T.S. Eliot's ideas into it, and that was very important to me.'

The EGOT-winning musical theatre composer and impresario Lloyd Webber had even higher praise for Taylor when he described her as being 'exactly the kind of talent who should write an original musical'. He said that he told her she should turn her sights to Broadway – and she agreed it was something she would like to do.

At the world premiere of "Cats" at Alice Tully Hall, Lincoln Center, December 16, 2019, New York City. Taylor played Bombalurina in this musical fantasy film

In the meantime she has contributed 13 songs to movie soundtracks including two for 2012's *The Hunger Games*, '*Sweeter than Fiction*' for the 2014 James Corden film *One Chance*, '*I Don't Wanna Live Forever*' for 2017's *Fifty Shades Darker*, which was Grammy nominated, and '*Carolina*' for 2022's adaptation of the novel *Where The Crawdads Sing*.

Her original documentary work include 2020's *Miss Americana* – a captivating portrait of her personal life at that time and a deep exploration of her career. The film pulled back the curtain to reveal Taylor's highs and lows, including exhilarating moments of success, to her struggles with self-doubt and public scrutiny. Using candid interviews and behind-the-scenes footage, Taylor shared with fans how she grappled with the pressures of fame, navigated complex industry dynamics, and confronted her own insecurities.

One of the documentary's most compelling aspects was Taylor's willingness to tackle difficult topics head-on. From her experiences with body image issues to her decision to speak out about politics, the documentary showed a brave and unapologetic side of Taylor that fans had rarely seen before.

But amidst the challenges, there were also moments of real triumph and resilience. Fans witnessed Taylor finding her voice, standing up for herself and her beliefs, and ultimately embracing her role as a powerful advocate for change.

Taylor Swift gives an interview at the Grammy Nominee Party at Lowes Vanderbilt Hotel, January 22, 2008, Nashville, Tennessee

Taylor: Icon of our times

Next, Taylor directed and appeared in her own short film, a romantic drama all timed to the 10-minute fan favourite *All Too Well*. Screened at the Toronto International Film Festival, *All Too Well: The Short Film*, starred Sadie Sink and Dylan O'Brien as a couple whose tempestuous relationship breaks up, partly because of their age gap. It included an appearance from Taylor playing 'Her, Later On' – the older version of Sadie Sink's character. The film was critically acclaimed and won Taylor a Grammy for Best Music Video 2023 and the Best Video and the Best Direction prize at the 2022 MTV Video Music Awards.

Taylor has since hinted at a full-blown directorial debut to come.

With so many skills and abilities outside of music, Taylor can pick and choose her projects – so perhaps Hollywood will prove to be a big draw for her.

Attending the "All Too Well" premiere at the AMC Lincoln Square in New York City, November 12, 2021

Taylor:

:: Taylor: Icon of our times

Her brand

The way Taylor's career is going has no contemporary precedent. That's partly because she has always been an absolute force of nature. She's insanely talented for sure, but as that's never enough on its own, she was lucky to be blessed with great focus, resilience, persistence, stamina, and a love of hard work.

Her unparalleled success is also because her musical talents are balanced by her skills in business, including great acuity around the 21st century's essential marketing tools of social media and brand management.

Taylor's rise to stardom coincided with the emergence of new social media channels and she became masterful in managing this new media. Becoming tech-savvy undoubtedly gave Taylor a head start in generating audiences for her early work. Such business sense was likely inherited from her parents Scott and Andrea who were both successful financiers - Scott had his own investment banking operation linked to Merrill Lynch and Andrea was marketing manager for an investment fund. Their expertise in marketing and money came into its own when, in 2002, they began to realise that their daughter was serious about a career in music and were quick off the mark to make the most of the burgeoning internet and its relatively infant social media platforms by creating a MySpace page for her.

Scott Swift, Taylor Swift and Andrea Swift arrive at Narita International Airport on May 31, 2014 in Narita, Japan

Scott and Andrea were by no means tiger parents, but they believed in their daughter and backed her to the hilt, even going as far as relocating the family to Nashville in 2003 to help further her career. They were also smart enough to secure *taylorswift.com* as a website address back in the mid-2000s, complete with download links to a selection of her songs – some of her own, plus a few covers.

Taylor: Her brand

MySpace

In the late 2000s MySpace (now Myspace) was the largest social networking site in the world and played an important part in promoting the pop culture and music of its time through its viral sharing capabilities. From 2005, following the launch of YouTube, users could embed videos into their profiles. By the late 2010s the site had been sold and subsumed by other corporations having lost out to rival platform Facebook in terms of appeal and users.

But, for a brief moment in time, Myspace was more than just a website—it was a community, a cultural hub, and a reflection of the digital zeitgeist. Though it may have faded into obscurity, its impact on the internet and popular culture was huge. Along with other now defunct sites such as Friendster and Bebo, it serves as a reminder of the ever-changing landscape of the digital world.

Taylor Swift opening for Brad Paisley in 2007 to promote her first album

Since then, Taylor has become an expert at leveraging social media to promote her brand, as well of course of skilfully using social media to promote her music and upcoming projects.

In fact she blazed the trail for the ultimate album rollout experience. Things typically kick off with her dropping cryptic clues and countdowns which are eagerly decoded by her devotees.

Her elaborate social media campaigns also include teasers for lyric videos, often leading to full-blown cinematic masterpieces packed with references and 'easter eggs' for die-hard Swifties to crack. It's a shrewd promotional tactic, demonstrating Taylor's unique ability to generate buzz and anticipation, turning each new release into a cultural event. In the run up to new material, her interviews, and music videos are strewn with clues as she continues to play games with her fans who love collecting information and piecing it all together to identify anything and everything from a new song, to a lyric or the subject of a track.

Taylor teased her eagerly awaited re-recorded first album like a seasoned sleuth, sprinkling clues left, right and centre during a time of already feverish anticipation for the Reputation (TV) release.

Taylor Swift performing the national anthem before the Philadelphia Phillies take on the Tampa Bay Rays in game three of the 2008 MLB World Series, October 25, 2008

For example, within the fandom - where every album has its own colour - green or teal is generally associated with her debut album *Taylor Swift*. Fans have also deduced that Taylor will often signal what is going on in her life through her outfit choices. So even something as seemingly innocent (to a non-Swiftie) as wearing green socks, which Taylor has done recently, is seized upon and analysed as a potential reference to that album, which the fans call Debut (TV).

Fans revel in the game, which they liken to a grown up treasure hunt, even starting a meme craze around the phrase 'Debutation'.

Taylor: Her brand

However, Taylor's social media prowess is about so much more than publicity and promotion—it's also about forging genuine connections with her audience. Whether she's giving fans a peek into her life, chatting directly with followers, or unveiling her latest music in unique ways, Taylor has crafted an online presence that's as influential as it is personal. Through her authentic approach, she has not only cemented her status as a musical icon but has also become a beacon of connection in the digital age, proving that being relatable is just as important as being talented. Commentators have described this interactive fanship as Taylor's own 'metaverse'.

Yet how is it possible for Taylor to remain relatable when she's the most famous woman alive, living a life completely different to that of her fans. That surely comes down to her music. Despite her celebrity status and glamorous lifestyle, her lyrics still touch on universal and meaningful themes like love, heartbreak, and self-discovery, which strike a chord with listeners from all walks of life.

Secondly, there's the generational connection. Millennials grew up alongside Taylor and as they experienced the ups and downs of adolescence and young adulthood, Taylor was there, singing about similar experiences and emotions. Her songs feel like a soundtrack to their lives, creating a sense of shared journey and understanding. Now Gen-Zers have joined the party, having discovered her during the pandemic when TikTok was flooded with 'Swiftonian' content as she released her albums *folklore* and *evermore*. This new generation of fans found solace and connection in her songs, particularly during the strange time period of a world lockdown.

Overall Taylor has become a guiding light for many, women in particular, as they navigate their own journeys of growth and self-discovery.

Taylor Swift and Cat are seen in Soho on September 16, 2014 in New York City

Of course Taylor isn't just making music; in recent years she's set about rewriting the rules of the industry. In an industry where artists have too often felt at the mercy of record labels, Taylor has led the field in taking back control and reshaping the way tracks are owned and shared.

Taylor's well-publicised dispute with her former record label, Big Machine, brought the issue of artists' ownership of their work to the forefront.

When Big Machine sold the rights to her master recordings without her consent, Taylor took matters into her own hands. She had the genius idea of re-recording her early albums, not just to regain ownership, but to assert her authority over her music. As she told *Billboard* magazine in an interview for their Woman of the Decade cover story: 'Every week, we get a dozen synch requests to use *Shake It Off* in some advertisement or *Blank Space* in some movie trailer, and we say no to every single one of them.

'And the reason I'm rerecording my music ... is because I do want my music to live on. I do want it to be in movies, I do want it to be in commercials. But I only want that if I own it.'

But then she had the ingenious idea of boosting these new albums with the 'From the Vault' concept. Each re-recorded album includes a handful of tracks fans won't have heard before. It's like uncovering buried treasure: Taylor digs into her archives, dusts off previously unreleased songs, and gifts them to her fans. These tracks, which have been tucked away from the spotlight for years, offer a fascinating glimpse into her creative process and evolution.

Taylor: Her brand

Taylor Swift performs at the 43rd Annual Country Music Association Awards in Nashville, Tennessee on November 11, 2009

But this isn't just about releasing forgotten tunes. It's a statement—a bold declaration of artistic freedom. By sharing these hidden gems Taylor is reclaiming control and deepening her connection with her audience at the same time.

Taylor Swift performs during the 1989 World Tour at Levi's Stadium on August 15, 2015, in Santa Clara, California

Taylor Swift performs onstage during the 2019 American Music Awards at the Microsoft Theate on November 24, 2019, in Los Angeles, California

Taylor's albums re-released so far:

Fearless – Taylor's Version
Released in April 2021 with six new tracks 'From the Vaults'.

Red – Taylor's Version
Released in November 2021 with nine 'Vaults' tracks, although only six had never been heard before.

Speak Now – Taylor's Version
Released in July 2023 with six 'Vaults' tracks.

1989 – Taylor's Version
Released in October 2023 with five 'Vaults' tracks.

Lover, released in 2019 under the Republic Records label, was the first album Taylor fully owned.

In keeping with her playful approach to fan interactions, Taylor likes to sprinkle clues about these re-releases. Signs that *Reputation* (Taylor's Version) was on the way included Taylor making her Instagram picture black and white, and wearing black and white (the theme of the album) to the 2024 Grammys. She also parted her hair very deeply to the side and chose red lips – both choices reminiscent of her look back then – which sent fans into a whirl, believing she was signalling the re-recorded album's release.

The grand finale of her re-recording extravaganza will be her first album 'Taylor Swift (Taylor's Version)' affectionately known as '*Debut (TV)*' by die-hard fans.

For the newer Swifties who joined the fandom during Taylor's pop star era, the excitement for "Debut (TV)" might not match the fervour that was around "1989 (TV)" or "Rep (TV)." Yet, for the OGs, it's a nostalgic journey they can't wait to take. Many have long been desperate for Taylor to revisit the country tunes of her early days. While she's treated audiences to some of these Nashville classics during her Eras Tour's 'surprise tracks' segment, there will be a special magic in hearing them anew, sung in Taylor's fully matured voice.

For fans, it's like getting an exclusive backstage pass to Swift's creative world. These unreleased tracks are a treasure trove of emotion, showing the raw talent and authenticity that fans have come to love.

Taylor Swift attends the 66th Grammy Awards styled with her hair parted to the side and bold red lips

In a music industry where profit often trumps artistic integrity, Taylor's approach is refreshing. She's proving that it's possible to thrive on your own terms, without sacrificing creative control. With every 'From the Vault' release, Taylor is not just rewriting her own narrative; she's setting a new standard for artists everywhere.

Even before she had the need to regain ownership of her music, Taylor was an early advocate for musicians everywhere as she changed and shaped the business model that music streaming platforms use. To this end, Taylor has frequently and coherently outlined her belief that music should not be free.

Vinyl records and CDs of 1989 Taylor's Version are seen on sale at the HMV store on Oxford Street, London, December 2023. Taylor famously withheld the original version of 1989 from Spotify

Taylor: Icon of our times

By 2014, some years into her career, the whole music industry began changing fast with physical album sales declining as digital downloads and streaming came in.

The first hint of her views on the digital landscape came in an article she wrote for the *Wall Street Journal* in July 2014 headlined, 'For Taylor Swift, the Future of Music Is a Love Story'. In a generally positive piece about the music industry, Taylor included a section about her belief that music should be paid for.

'Music is art, and art is important and rare', she wrote. 'Important, rare things are valuable. Valuable things should be paid for. It's my opinion that music should not be free, and my prediction is that individual artists and their labels will someday decide what an album's price point is. I hope they don't underestimate themselves or undervalue their art.'

Taylor felt strongly that she needed to take a stand over her rights as an artist. 'The landscape of the music industry itself is changing so quickly, that everything new, like Spotify, all feels to me a bit like a grand experiment. I'm not willing to contribute my life's work to an experiment that I don't feel fairly compensates the writers, producers, artists, and creators of this music," she said.

Backing her words with actions, Taylor made headlines by withholding her chart-topping 1989 album and withdrawing her entire back catalogue from Spotify, citing her disagreement with their ad-supported, free service model which she believed gave her music away for free and undermined the premium service that offered higher royalties for songwriters.

She followed this up by taking on the massive and influential Apple Music organisation. Aged just 25, Taylor posted an open letter to the tech giant Apple Music on her Tumblr page that made waves throughout the industry.

The letter outlined her disagreement with Apple's policy of withholding artist royalties during the three-month trial period consumers were offered on their music platform. Taylor simply wasn't having it and told Apple that her smash-hit album *1989* would be withheld from their platform until they changed their policy. Apple listened. They swiftly reversed their payment policy, all thanks to Taylor's outspoken challenge.

By speaking out against the idea of giving music away for free and controlling access to her material by streaming services, Taylor helped shape how the new world of digital music works.

After making her views known, she re-added her catalogue, plus 1989, to Spotify and other digital streaming platforms in 2017.

It must have therefore been super-sweet when Apple Music named her its Artist of the Year for 2023. She was not only the most-streamed female artist in Apple Music's history, but also the female artist with the most songs appearing on the platform's Global Daily Top 100.

That same year Spotify announced her as its most-streamed artist globally, on reaching over 26.1 billion streams and beating Bad Bunny's three-year record.

The final pillar supporting Taylor's brand is live performance - predominantly her staggeringly successful tours.

Taylor: Her brand

Taylor Swift performs live on stage during the 1989 World Tour at Lanxess Arena on June 20, 2015, in Cologne, Germany

Each one is a meticulously crafted spectacle, where every element, from stage design to costumes, contributes to a larger narrative. Taylor doesn't just perform concerts; she creates immersive journeys for her fans.

From her earliest days as a teenage singer she always enjoyed performing live and was determined to enjoy herself – which she knew would only happen if she was happy with her show. Having always set high standards for herself it was natural that, when she became big enough to headline, her tours would be no exception. As she has told journalists many times, 'I love being onstage. It's one of my favourite things in the world.'

Taylor's first headlining tour, Fearless, came in 2009 and played in 52 cities through the US and Canada, Europe, Japan and Australia, reaching an audience of over one million people. Despite these huge audiences Taylor endeavoured to keep some intimacy by moving about within each venue, performing in different locations throughout the evening, so she could get up close and personal with the crowd. The concerts were increasingly theatrical, including lots of scenes and costume changes. Taylor even included simulated 'rain' on stage and got drenched while singing *Should've Said No*.

After the release of her third album, Taylor embarked on her Speak Now World Tour, visiting 17 countries across Asia, Europe, North America, and Australasia between February 2011 and March 2012. Again scenery, costume and production values were high and theatrical, with Taylor enchanting audiences by creating moments of genuine spontaneity which her fans loved.

It was another massive success with critics praising everything from its sheer visual impact to Taylor's performance and connection with the audience. Many of the tracks on this album were perfect for performance in the big arenas Taylor was now able to command. It became the highest-grossing female and solo tour of 2011, with worldwide earnings of over $150 million.

Earnings and audiences kept growing with the Red Tour of 2013-2014 – another whirlwind of sold out arenas, dazzling costumes and unforgettable moments. Yet the Red Tour wasn't just a musical triumph; it was another financial powerhouse making, Taylor, at the tender age of 25, one of the highest-grossing touring artists of all time.

But she wasn't done yet. Back on stage between May and December 2015 for her record-breaking run of 85 shows on her *1989* World Tour, Taylor now picked up the records for the best attended tour of all time, the highest grossing of that year and, eventually, that decade.

Taylor Swift and her mother as she wins the 50th Anniversary Milestone Award for Youngest ACM Entertainer of the Year, during the 50th Academy of Country Music Awards, 2015

Taylor: Her brand

By the time her Reputation tour kicked off in 2018, Taylor only had her own records and standards to beat – which she did and has continued to do with her global Eras Tour – the highest-grossing tour of all time and the first ever to surpass the $1 billion mark in revenue.

Its success created a financial phenomenon known as the Taylor Swift effect, or Swiftonomics. When Taylor's show rolls into town it brings incredible revenue in its wake. The 53 U.S. cities alone where Taylor played are estimated to have added $4.3 billion to the economy.

Industry pollsters estimated that the tour could generate $5 billion, and the U.S. Federal Reserve – the country's central banking system – has confirmed that cities hosting the Eras Tour get a huge economic boost when Taylor is in town.

This is rarified territory for an artist to get into and brings a level of legitimacy to what could in the past have been dismissed as frivolous fun for fans.

While tour ticket sales are a big part of her revenue, other streams include VIP packages, merchandise, sponsorship and strategic brand partnerships.

Taylor Swift performs onstage during the 2018 Reputation Stadium Tour at Soldier Field on June 1, 2018 in Chicago, Illinois

But then Taylor made a move which redefined what it means to be a successful touring artist. She produced a concert film of her Eras Tour which, within weeks, became the all-time highest grossing concert/documentary picture ever, beating Michael Jackson's 2009 *'This Is It'*.

Released in cinemas worldwide in October 2023, *Taylor Swift: The Eras Tour* was a box office smash, with advance ticket sales alone surpassing $100m (£82m). It has since gone on to make over $260 million in global revenue and earn 11th place in the IMDb rankings for the top 20 highest-grossing films of the year in the US.

Billed as a "breathtaking, cinematic view" of her concerts, it was recorded in August 2023 during a series of shows at Sofi Stadium in Inglewood, California, US. In a further example of her pioneering approach, Taylor struck a groundbreaking distribution deal directly with American movie theatre chain AMC Theaters, bypassing the traditional route of partnering with a film studio.

The film's success boosted Taylor's standing in the music business to the extent that she beat every executive in her industry to take the top spot in the 2024 Billboard Power List – a prestigious ranking of the most influential and powerful people in the music industry. It's unheard of for an artist to do this.

Additionally, in October 2023, financial analytics and media conglomerate Bloomberg declared Taylor was a billionaire with a US$1.1bn fortune boosted by her Eras tour, its accompanying movie, and the 'Taylor's Version' re-recordings of her albums.

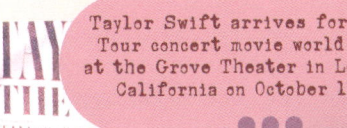

Taylor Swift arrives for the Eras Tour concert movie world premiere at the Grove Theater in Los Angeles, California on October 11, 2023.

Taylor: Her brand

Taylor Swift performs onstage for night one of the Eras Tour at GEHA Field at Arrowhead Stadium on July 7, 2023, in Kansas City, Missouri

Taylor: Icon of our times

With other music royalties adding to the rising value of her music catalogue, Taylor's 'Billionaire' era had begun. When prestigious business magazine *Forbes* published its 2023 World's Billionaires List in April 2024, Taylor featured for the first time at #14 with a net worth of $1.1 billion.

Taylor is one of only four contemporary musicians ever to have achieved billionaire status (the others being Rihanna, Beyoncé, and Jay-Z) and has made history as the first to have reached the milestone from songwriting and performing alone. The others boosted their fortunes by diversifying into business ventures outside the music industry, such as beauty and fashion.

Taylor has never touted herself as an executive in the traditional sense. Yet by executing some of the music industry's most daring and triumphant business strategies ever, she has become a very savvy businesswoman, now wielding huge power in her industry where she also dominates as a phenomenally creative artist. She sets the bar for innovation, showing the industry the level of commitment needed to tackle the major challenges that lie ahead of it.

In an interview with *Billboard* to mark her topping their power list, Taylor explained some of her thinking about business, saying, "The biggest crossroads moments of my career came down to sticking to my instincts when my ideas were looked at with scepticism. When someone says to me, 'But that has never been done successfully before,' it fires me up. We have to take strategic risks every day in this industry, but every once in a while, you have to really trust your gut and take a flying leap. My re-recordings are my favourite example of this, and I'm extremely grateful to my team and fans for taking that leap with me because it absolutely changed my life."

Taylor:

Taylor: Icon of our times

Her fans

Taylor has one of most diehard and devoted fan bases on the planet. It's largely this profound personal and emotional connection with her fans that propelled her from mere superstar to a revered figure with almost cult-like status.

From her earliest days back in Nashville, Taylor has been famously accessible to her fans, the 'Swifties'. Understanding that many fans see her as being almost like an elder sister, Taylor has tried to stay as personally connected to them as possible. Ever since setting up her *MySpace* page and personally blogging when she was a teenager, she has maintained direct links with them through her social media as well as face to face.

From her very early days as a teenage talent Taylor set about modernising and rebooting the country music tradition of telling stories about longing and regret. In doing so she engaged and energised a new generation of young women who are always touched by her often confessional lyrics and narrative themes.

Her second album, *Fearless*, which began redefining the teen-pop genre, included songs with strong narratives as Taylor drew on her real-life experiences, which at that point were about issues facing teenage girls including romance and heartbreak. Many of her lyrics sounded not unlike diary entries.

'I write as life happens to me,' Taylor confirmed in an interview with *Rolling Stone* in 2010.

Taylor: Icon of our times

13 is Taylor's lucky number. She paints it on her hand before a show and so do her fans.

Taylor: Her fans

It was back in those early days, when she was aged around 14, that Taylor says she began dropping cryptic clues into her music. In an interview years later with US television talk show host Jimmy Fallon, Taylor explained how she wanted to do something that incentivised fans to read the lyrics because '....my lyrics are what I'm most proud of out of everything I do, every aspect of my job.

'In my lyrics, for my first several albums, I would have all lower case letter lyrics, except for capital letters every once in a while ....which spelled out a secret code, a secret passage... or told them a story about the album or a hint about what the song was about.

Taylor Swift has always had a close-knit relationship with younger brother Austin

'When it got out of control was when I started to realise that it wasn't just me that had fun with this, that they [her fans] had fun with it too. Then I couldn't stop. All I started thinking of was how do I hint at things? How far is too far in advance? Can I hint at something three years in advance? Can I even plan things out that far? I think I'm going to try to do it!

'The first time I did a crazy thing like that was with the video for *Look What You Made Me Do*. I started playing with doing nods to former musical eras I've been in in my career and all kinds of weird stuff for them to just go through and ask '…what does that mean?!'

'I think it is perfectly reasonable for people to be normal music fans and to have a normal relationship to music but if you want to go down a rabbit hole with us, come along, the water's great, jump in… we're all mad here.'

So mad in fact that fans now analyse every song, every dance, every post which might reveal some information. Fans can now put themselves inside Taylor's world in a way that was simply unimaginable 20 years ago.

Swifties' fan theories on the inspiration and meaning of her songs can be next level. During the run up to the release of Taylor's 11th album *The Tortured Poets Department* in April 2024, fans pored over the pre-released track list looking for clues as to the album's theme.

Pondering over the possible meaning of the track *loml* as an acronym they came up with love of my life, loss of my life, losing only my love and living only my life – you get the idea!

When Taylor talked about the album during an Eras Tour concert in Australia in February 2024, fans became convinced it was about her breakup with actor boyfriend Joe Alwyn. 'I needed to make it. It was really a lifeline for me,' Taylor said. 'It sort of reminded me of why songwriting is something that actually gets me through life.' This statement, coupled with the release of track titles including *I Can Fix Him* and *So Long London* (where she and Londoner Alwyn had a home) gave further credence to fan claims. Then the fact that Alwyn once mentioned in an interview that he was part of a WhatsApp group chat called Tortured Man Club, and Taylor going on to create five Apple Music playlists based on the five stages of grief: (denial, anger, bargaining, depression, and acceptance), bolstered the theories around TTPD further still.

Alongside 'messaging' her fans, Taylor has always made a point of getting up close and personal with them as much as possible, before, during, and after shows, signing autographs, sending presents, handing out hugs, and throwing bracelets from the stage.

Taylor Swift's former boyfriend Joe Alwyn

But she's occasionally gone to even more effort than that. She once surprised a Swiftie by coming to his wedding and performing a super-special stripped-back rendition of *Blank Space,* accompanying herself at the piano. She's also popped up at a bridal shower and been known to surprise fans at their homes or events, often after seeing their posts on social media. A deep dive into Swifties' social media accounts reveals varied examples of her generosity towards them, as she does everything from visit them in hospital to helping pay off their college tuition fees, like a modern day fairy godmother.

Taylor Swift poses for photos with fans as she arrives at the 26th Annual ARIA Awards, November 29, 2012 in Sydney, Australia

Through these often spontaneous visits, Taylor keeps up the connection with her fans on a personal level and shows her appreciation for their support. She clearly recognises that she is a role model to young women and takes that responsibility very seriously.

Then of course there have been the 'Secret Sessions' where Taylor has invited fans to her home for an album preview. These are meet and greets to beat all meet and greets. The first of these was in 2014 for *1989* and similar sessions followed for *Reputation* and *Lover*. Taylor personally selected the Swifties who were invited by, as she put it, 'cyber-stalking' their socials to identify the most devoted and deserving.

For the *1989* events there were 89 invites to each of a series of sessions in the autumn of 2014, held at Taylor's homes in New York, Los Angeles and Rhode Island, plus another at her mother's home in Nashville and one in a London hotel.

The fans knew they had been chosen for a Taylor Swift event but had no idea what was actually awaiting them.

In a video of the first session, held on 20 September 2014 in Los Angeles, Taylor is seen baking chocolate chip and toasted coconut cookies and peeking out of a window excitedly as the fans arrived.

In a piece to camera she explained, 'This is the first of the secret sessions which are little mini living room house parties where I'm going to be playing my fans the album first. So we wanted to surprise them. They're here, they're out mingling and eating and things like that. They know something is going on but I don't know if they think *this* is going on!'

Taylor: Her fans

Taylor Swift autographs for 13 hours on June 13, 2010, in Nashville, Tennessee, at the CMA Music Festival

Taylor's every stage performance somehow bridges the gap between her fans and herself. In the early days on the brink of fame, when she was still able to walk through the audience, she would give out hugs galore which really cemented her connection with fans. Around that time she also began developing what is almost a secret shared language with Swifties using her lucky number 13, making her heart gesture with her fingers and developing her now much-memed 'surprised' face in response to the reactions of her audience. She celebrated this rare connection with her fans in the 2010 track *Long Live* on *Speak Now* which

reflected on her career so far and her relationship with her team – including as she explained on her website, '...my band, and my producer, and all the people who have helped us build this brick by brick. The fans, the people who I feel that we are all in this together, this song talks about the triumphant moments that we've had in the last two years.

'This song for me is like looking at a photo album of all the award shows, and all the stadium shows, and all the hands in the air in the crowd. It's sort of the first love song that I've written to my team.' Whenever she sings the line 'the crowds in stands went wild' the fans know their part and scream back at her.

Taylor Swift brought her Red Tour back to the New York market, playing a sold-out show to more than 55,000 fans at MetLife Stadium on July 13, 2013, in East Rutherford, New Jersey

Taylor Swift performing during her Fearless Tour

Taylor: Icon of our times

122

Nowadays as Taylor performs in huge stadiums to tens of thousands of fans at a time, she still works hard to create a connection with the crowd, the real intentional inclusion is palpable. Amid all the razzmatazz come quiet moments of stunning intimacy, particularly when she sits alone at her piano. When she talks to the audience it's like they are her friends who just popped in for a chat. She seems devoted to fan service and has become skilled at presenting two versions of herself: one being a private individual and the other her celebrity persona.

In return the Swifties are fiercely loyal, queuing for hours for tickets, flooding social media sites if she needs support, poring over her every post, calculating clues – however subtle - that help with song interpretations or creative choices. There are always countless fan theories online, including many around the 'Taylor's Version' album re-releases, songs added to or omitted from the Eras set list, while other strands run around unravelling lyrics, her clothing choices, and her hair and makeup styles. Outside of the particular, there are endless online discussions about all the lore that surrounds Taylor generally.

Taylor Swift performs onstage at the 54th Annual Grammy Awards in 2012

Taylor's Most Talked About Tracks

Taylor's discography is rich with songs that have prompted intense analysis and speculation among fans. Here is a rundown of some of her most talked about tracks ...

All Too Well

This song from the *Red* album is often interpreted as one of Taylor's most personal and emotionally charged songs. It's widely believed to be inspired by her past relationship with actor Jake Gyllenhaal, which reportedly ended in 2011. The song vividly depicts the aftermath of a breakup, capturing feelings of heartbreak, longing, and nostalgia.

The song's detailed storytelling and evocative imagery has led fans to speculate about the real-life events that inspired it. From the mention of a scarf left behind, to the imagery of autumn leaves, every lyric paints a vivid picture of heartache and reflection.

Additionally, the bridge of *All Too Well* is particularly powerful, with Taylor singing about a moment when she thought the relationship was strong and genuine, only to realise later that it was falling apart. This section, in particular, resonates with fans who have experienced the sudden realisation that a relationship was not as perfect as it seemed and suffered similar feelings of betrayal and emotional turmoil.

Dear John

Found on the *Speak Now* album, this song is rumoured to be about Taylor's past relationship with her ex-boyfriend and fellow singer-songwriter John Mayer. Fans analyse the lyrics for clues about their romance and debate its significance in Taylor's discography. Taylor was just 19 when she began a relationship with Mayer, who was more than 10 years her senior at 32. The couple dated for just under a year and following their break-up – one of Taylor's firsts– she wrote this track which reportedly left him 'humiliated'. He's also thought to have been the inspiration for other songs including *Ours, Superman,* and *The Story of Us.*

Taylor Swift playing a sold-out crowd of over 51,000 fans on her Speak Now World Tour at Lincoln Financial Field in her home state of Pennsylvania

Bad Blood

From the *1989* album, Bad Blood sparked controversy due to rumours that it was about Taylor's feud with fellow artist Katy Perry. The pair reportedly fell out over a dispute involving backup dancers, which escalated into a public disagreement.

The speculation gained traction due to interviews and public statements made by both artists, as well as subtle hints in their respective songs and social media posts.

Then, when the song's accompanying music video came out featuring an ensemble cast of celebrities, including Taylor's close friends, the speculation was refuelled. Some fans theorised that the video was a deliberate message to Katy Perry, showcasing Taylor's support network and portraying a sense of unity among her friends.

Taylor has never confirmed the true inspiration behind the song, and it may indeed simply be about broader themes of betrayal and conflict. However the ongoing speculation adds an extra layer of mystery to the track, solidifying its place as one of Taylor's most intriguing.

Taylor Swift performs tracks from her 1989 album during the 2015 iHeartRadio Music Awards

Out of the Woods

Given the timing of its release and the lyrical content, fans were in little doubt that this track from *1989* revolved around Taylor's relationship with her ex-boyfriend and fellow superstar, the musician Harry Styles.

There was general agreement that the lyrics reflected the emotional turmoil of a relationship characterised by highs and lows. Its vivid narrative imagery, including references to crashing cars and escaping wolves, prompted speculation about the metaphorical meanings behind these symbols. Some interpreted them as representing the dangers and obstacles faced in relationships, while others viewed them as symbols of emotional vulnerability and resilience.

Overall fans were encouraged to note that Taylor seemed to be looking for ways of overcoming obstacles and finding the clarity that would empower her, despite the failure of her relationship with Styles.

Look What You Made Me Do

This lead single from the *Reputation* album sparked a flurry of fan theories and speculation. Its darker tone and pointed lyrics, led many to conclude it was inspired by Taylor's much publicised disputes with Kanye West and Kim Kardashian – a furore that blew up after West interrupted Taylor's acceptance speech at the 2009 MTV Video Music Awards.

A prevalent theory was that the track marked the beginning of Taylor's reputation redemption arc. The song's lyrics and imagery were interpreted as Taylor confronting her critics and reclaiming control of her narrative after facing public scrutiny and controversies.

Some fans went even further, taking the track as evidence that Taylor was adopting a new persona or at least a persona shift, particularly as its accompanying video featured various iterations of her from past music videos and public appearances.

The video was also packed with symbolism and Easter eggs, leading to further speculation about hidden messages and meanings. Fans dissected every frame of the video, analysing references to Taylor's past controversies, relationships, and career milestones.

Kanye West jumps onstage after Taylor Swift won the Best Female Video award during the 2009 MTV Video Music Awards at Radio City Music Hall on September 13, 2009, in New York City

Taylor: Her fans

The Last Great American Dynasty

Featured on the *folklore* album, this song tells the story of Rebekah Harkness, a prominent socialite and a previous real-life owner of Taylor's Rhode Island mansion. The song is packed with historical references and has inspired a wealth of fan theories and interpretations, which all goes to show how skilfully Taylor can weave complex narratives that resonate on multiple levels. Rebekah Harkness had a colourful life story and a reputation for rebellious behaviour and lavish parties. Yet the song portrays Rebekah as a misunderstood figure who faced a backlash from society for defying traditional gender roles. This has led some fans to interpret the track as a feminist commentary on Rebekah's life and the societal expectations placed on women.

Others speculate that *The Last Great American Dynasty* contains parallels to Taylor's own experiences with fame and public scrutiny. By juxtaposing Rebekah's story with her own, Taylor could be exploring themes of identity, belonging, and the pressures of celebrity life.

Another strand of discussion interprets the song's lyrics metaphorically, with Rebekah as a symbol of rebellion and nonconformity. The 'holiday house' mentioned could represent a sanctuary where people are free to express themselves without judgment or societal constraints.

Taylor Swift reacts to winning the Album of the Year award for *folklore* during the 63rd Annual Grammy Awards

Being a Swiftie means following Taylor's lead in really being who you are, feeling what you feel and, most importantly, celebrating the changes and stages that life throws at you.

The more fans study Taylor's journey, the more her work makes sense to them. They admire her remarkable ability to turn any unwarranted negativity directed at her into a force for good, enabling her to transcend pettiness, jealousy, and unkind or unethical behaviour.

Her most ardent fans, those who really identify with Taylor, and especially those of a similar age who essentially grew up with her, follow her to the point that they have almost modelled their lives on her. They will emulate her fashion looks, share her likes and dislikes, advocate for causes she believes in, use her music as inspiration for their own creative endeavours, and form connections with other Swifties based on their shared admiration for Taylor.

Speaking in her 2020 autobiographical documentary *Miss Americana*, Taylor said of her fans, 'We feel like we grew up together...it's like they've been reading my diary.'

In 2018 fans had the opportunity to look at some of Taylor's old journals for real as she included photocopied pages of various handwritten diary entries, with the deluxe version of her album, *Lover*. The entries, all written between 2003 and 2017, included her cryptic thought, noted as being written in Nashville in August 2016, that 'This summer is the apocalypse'. Other entries referenced her secret romance with Joe Alwyn, as well as details about her long-standing feud with Kanye West.

You Belong with Me

A March 2023 survey by the Morning Consult decision intelligence company found that some **53% of American adults considered themselves to be fans of Taylor**, with **16% identifying themselves as 'avid' fans**.

Of avid fans, **44%** said they were **Swifties**.

45% of avid fans are millennials (people aged 27-42 years old), while 23% are baby boomers (over 60s), **21% are Gen Xers** (40-50 year olds) and **11% are Gen Z** (aged 26 and under).

Taylor Swift accepts the Song of the Year award for "Anti-Hero" during the 2023 iHeartRadio Music Awards at Dolby Theatre in Los Angeles, California on March 27, 2023

Taylor's social media game is next-level awesome. She doesn't just post updates; she creates a real bond with her fans, making them feel like they're right there beside her as part of her journey. It's like one big family, all thanks to Taylor's magic touch.

And let's talk about authenticity— which Taylor has in spades. There's no carefully curated content nor polished PR statements here. She's real, refreshingly candid and unfiltered, sharing her thoughts on everything from politics to the latest pop culture craze. Fans love her honesty and how she stays so relatable.

At times it's like having a backstage pass to her life and creativity. She's all about sharing those juicy behind-the-scenes moments— whether she's in the recording studio, sharing videos when she's at home with her cats Meredith, Olivia and Benjamin, or teasing us with sneak peeks of her latest music videos. It's like she's inviting fans into her world, showing us the real Taylor beyond the spotlight and the stage persona.

Taylor is all about keeping the conversation going with her fans. She doesn't just post and ghost—she's right there in the comments, showing her love and gratitude for their support. It's like she's building this community where everyone feels like they belong, and that's what keeps everyone coming back for more.

I Know Places

Fans' genuine emotional connection to Taylor through social media – a sociological phenomenon known as a parasocial relationship – has added a new dimension to the fan/celebrity dynamic.

The New York Times reported that, according to Alex Kresovich, a doctoral student at the University of North Carolina's Hussman School of Journalism and Media who has published research on parasocial relationships, 'The feelings people have with media persona are nearly indistinguishable from their friends in real life'.

It's not that these 'super fans' don't have their own friends – they certainly do – but merely that, while everyone forms such relationships with celebrities whom they admire to some degree, it's a more intense relationship when the celebrity is able to respond as Taylor does. Humans have an innate drive to connect with each other and Taylor's genuine interest in her fans, who she is always quick to credit for her success, simply builds on this.

Taylor: Her fans

Taylor Swift performs during her Eras Tour

When the 18 years of connection between artist and fan reached an apex on the Eras Tour it was about so much more than the music—it was about the memories. It was about revelling in nostalgia, dancing and singing and feeling recognised and special in a way only Taylor can achieve. It's a tour that will forever hold a special place in the hearts of Swifties everywhere, reminding them why they fell in love with Taylor in the first place and enjoying the liberation - almost the licence - Taylor gives them to celebrate their own 'past eras' rather than feel ashamed or regretful over anything about them.

In addition to her many other records and accolades, Taylor can hold close the fact that she has single-handedly revolutionised the relationship between artist and fan.

Friendship bracelet frenzy

Thanks to Taylor, friendship bracelets are back in the spotlight. Fans are trading these colourful beaded tokens like crazy at her live shows —arriving armed with stacks of them to swap with fellow Swifties.

But where did this blast from the past come from, and why are fans going wild for it? Friendship bracelets have been around forever, with roots tracing back to Indigenous communities in Central and South America, they later became a hit among hippies in the 1970s and school kids in the 1990s.

Each one is a tiny work of art, made from braided string and beads, and given to friends as a sign of their close bond.

So, what's the Swiftie twist? Said to have been inspired by a lyric in her 2022 track *You're on Your Own, Kid*, Swiftie bracelets are like mini masterpieces, adorned with alphabet beads spelling out lyrics or inside jokes from Taylor's world. Fans are DIY-ing these tokens like there's no tomorrow, flooding social media with tutorials and displaying their creations to rack up views.

Squads of Swifties get together for pre-show bracelet-making parties, swapping tips and tricks like it's a crafting convention. And if you're part of the Swiftie community, you can join online groups dedicated to sharing bracelet inspiration and outfit ideas—it's like a whole new world of creativity and connection, all thanks to Taylor.

Taylor: Her fans

Friendship bracelets became a large part of Taylor Swift's concerts

Bringing Taylor's tour to life

2,200 Swifties were handpicked to join Taylor at the premiere of *Taylor Swift: The Eras Tour* concert film; held in Los Angeles on 11 October 2023.

'The capturing of the memories of this tour was so special because of what you brought to it,' Taylor told her fans. 'Your passion, your sense of humour, your attention to detail, the amount that you prepared for it, the amount that you cared for it. That is what I hope you get from this – how much you brought this tour to life.'

Her mere presence at the NFL games she attends to support her boyfriend Travis Kelce of the Kansas City Chiefs, has increased viewership and attendance. More evidence that her fans like what she likes.

Overall this unique relationship between artist and fan seems to be based on mutual appreciation – the love and devotion from fans which made Taylor's teenage dreams of stardom and acclaim come true, has been richly reciprocated as she has written and performed the hundreds of songs which now provide the soundtrack to their lives.

Swiftmas

Taylor delighted a group of her super fans in 2014 by sending them Christmas presents she had personally chosen and wrapped. While most arrived via FedEx, Taylor delivered some of them in person.

Swiftmas, as the event became known, caused huge excitement throughout the Swiftie community and a video showing fan reactions to her gifts and visits received more than a million views on YouTube in a week.

Travis Kelce embraced by Taylor Swift in the aftermath of the Kansas City Chiefs' Super Bowl LVIII victory, 11 February 2024

Taylor:

Taylor: Icon of our times

140

Her values

With world fame, a billion dollars in the bank and millions and millions of followers (468 million across all platforms and counting) Taylor has a potent platform and a pressure to use it. She uses this power for good and is now famous for her unwavering commitment to her values and her fearless stance against sexism and discrimination of all types. She is also well known as an advocate for causes she believes in, such as feminism, LGBTQ+ rights, various other social justice issues and political engagement and activism.

But it has naturally taken Taylor a few years to find her feet and decide where best to exert her influence. Having first found fame as a 16-year-old teenager it naturally took Taylor some time to formalise her views and find the confidence to speak out about them.

Now that she's such a famously formidable advocate for women's rights and empowerment, known for her fearless take downs of any person or company who is disrespectful or sexist, it's strange to remember that things weren't always that way.

Taylor herself reflected on this in a 2019 interview with British Vogue magazine, when she discussed how her youth made her initially oblivious to sexism in the music business.

'I would hear people talk about sexism in the music industry, and I'd be like, I don't see it. I don't understand,' she told the magazine. 'Then I realized that was because I was a kid. Men in the industry saw me as a kid. I was a lanky, scrawny, overexcited young girl who reminded them more of their little niece or their daughter than a successful woman in business or a colleague.'

Taylor: Her values

Taylor Swift making her iconic heart hands sign while she performs with Def Leppard on stage during the 2009 CMT Music Awards

But she noticed attitudes toward her changing as she grew up and became a hugely successful artist. 'It's fine to infantilize a girl's success and say, "How cute that she's having some hit songs",' she said. "But the second it becomes formidable? As soon as I started playing stadiums — when I started to look like a woman — that wasn't as cool anymore.'

Taylor used the same interview to call out the double standards for men and women writing songs about love and relationships. She's been subject to reams of press coverage and speculation on social media accusing her of mining her romantic relationships for material for her music. 'Find me a time when they say that about a male artist,' she said.

Now, through her music, actions, and words, she continuously champions the idea that everyone deserves to be treated fairly and with respect, regardless of gender, race, or sexual orientation. Her songs often echo themes of self-confidence, independence, and resilience, inspiring millions around the world to embrace their authenticity and stand up for what they believe in.

Two young activists with a sign quoting Taylor Swift in France on March 8, 2024, to mark International Women's Rights Day

The Man

As ever, Taylor has used music to expand on her thoughts and she highlighted the particular career challenges and barriers women face in her track *The Man* from her *Lover* album.

By imagining her life from a male perspective, Taylor uses this feminist anthem to address the idea that while men are praised for being assertive, ambitious, and dominant, women are often expected to be submissive and accommodating, grateful for their success and content not to strive for more.

She knows exactly what she's talking about. Throughout her career, Taylor has battled sexist stereotypes hurled at her by the media, faced relentless scrutiny and unfair criticism, and been subjected to gender-based double standards that her male counterparts rarely encounter. However, instead of succumbing to these pressures, Taylor has boldly confronted them head-on.

One standout example is Taylor's courageous decision to take legal action against former radio DJ David Mueller, who she had accused of groping her during a meet and greet event in 2013 – a case that she won in August 2017.

Mueller had denied Taylor's allegations and sued her for defamation, claiming that her accusations had lost him his job.

Having always maintained that the assault had happened, Taylor was understandably keen to defend herself and so she countersued him for alleged assault and battery, requesting a token but symbolic $1 in damages as she wanted to make a point, not money. Taylor appeared in court to testify and the jury went on to rule in her favour. She responded with the following statement.

'I acknowledge the privilege that I benefit from in life, in society and in my ability to shoulder the enormous cost of defending myself in a trial like this. My hope is to help those whose voices should also be heard. Therefore, I will be making donations in the near future to multiple organisations that help sexual assault victims defend themselves'.

Taylor: Her values

As well as seeking justice for herself, Taylor's part in the trial also sent a powerful message about consent and the importance of holding perpetrators accountable for their actions. Her bravery sparked conversations about sexual assault and helped empower survivors to speak out against their abusers. It also appeared to embolden her to lend her voice to criticising all kinds of sexism and misogyny. She signed up to support the Times Up movement, aimed at addressing harassment, and made a donation to the Rape, Abuse & Incest National Network (RAINN) as part of Sexual Assault Awareness Month.

The national hotline for RAINN reported a 35% increase in calls over the weekend after she testified.

A message displaying lyrics from the Taylor Swift song "Ours" is displayed across the street from the civil case of Taylor Swift vs David Mueller at the Alfred A. Arraj Courthouse on August 14, 2017 in Denver, Colorado

Taylor is also a vocal ally and supporter of the LGBTQ+ community. From advocating for LGBTQ+ rights to speaking out against discrimination, Taylor consistently uses her platform to amplify marginalised voices and promote inclusivity. She's donated generously to LGBTQ+ organizations, spoken out against discriminatory legislation, and celebrated love in all its forms through her music and actions. Aware that actions can speak louder than words, Taylor cast trans model Laith Ashley as her love interest in the music video for *Midnight's Lavender Haze*. Laith publicly thanked Taylor for the opportunity, adding that he was in 'awe, inspired and hopeful' by her storytelling abilities. 'Thank you for being an ally. Representation matters, AND LOVE WILL ALWAYS WIN!' he wrote on Instagram.

Taylor Swift at the 27th Annual GLAAD Media Awards Show, Los Angeles, 2 April, 2016

In her 2019 single *You Need to Calm Down*, Taylor took a bold stand against homophobia and included a mention for the US LGBTQ rights organization GLAAD, which promoted a surge in their donations. The accompanying music video featured appearances from LGBTQ+ icons like Ellen DeGeneres, RuPaul and Adam Lambert. To top it off, the final frame implored viewers to sign her petition supporting the US's Equality Act, which aims to outlaw discrimination based on gender identity and sexual orientation.

A nod from Taylor in any direction can really make a difference and fans pay close attention whenever she has something to say. She holds an incredible amount of power – luckily coupled with the sense to use it well.

When she posted on Instagram encouraging her followers to register to vote she galvanised 35,000 people to register and 157,000 visits to the site – averaging 13,000 users every 30 minutes – 13 being a number Taylor would be especially proud to note. 'I've been so lucky to see so many of you guys at my US shows recently,' she wrote on her Insta story. 'I've heard you raise your voices and I know how powerful they are. Make sure you're ready to use them in our elections this year!' She then posted a link to register at Vote.org – a non-partisan non-profit organisation. Its CEO Andrea Hailey praised Taylor's involvement saying that despite being among the busiest people in the world she 'always has time to stand up for democracy, use her own voice and encourage her fans and followers to use theirs.'

Speaking out about politics is something that Taylor didn't fully embrace until 2018.

Until that time, and despite sharing so much with her fans over the years, she had chosen to stay silent about her personal and political views. From her early days as a young star, she had always had a genuinely wholesome, entirely non-threatening image and never sought out controversy. She and her team were always acutely aware of the value of her 'brand' which made her an attractive proposition for advertisers and earned her royalties on merchandise and endorsement deals with companies including Diet Coke, Keds and Cover Girl.

But as Taylor grew up she began to struggle with the advice she'd been given about keeping her personal opinions to herself. She realised that she could use her platform to further those topics about which she cared the most.

Taylor: Her values

With the political climate in America becoming increasingly fevered, and Taylor finding more confidence on the cusp of her fourth decade, she decided that she needed to speak out. She described it as having the 'masking tape' off her mouth. Ultimately, Taylor's decision to break her silence on politics was a significant moment in her career and a huge shift in her public persona.

A scene from the 2020 Miss Americana documentary shows the evolution well. In a tense and tearful exchange with her father about her wanting to endorse Democratic candidate Phil Bredesen during a keenly contested US senate campaign, Taylor said that she 'needed to be on the right side of history' and that if Bredesen didn't win, she would 'at least have tried'.

Taylor Swift is interviewed by Teen Vogue Style Features Director Andrew Bevan during the Taylor Swift for Keds style icons event

Explaining her actions, after she had endured some previous criticism over her previous silence around political issues, she explained that she had been '...reluctant to publicly voice my political opinions, but due to several events in my life and in the world in the past two years, I feel very differently about that now.

'I always have and always will cast my vote based on which candidate will protect and fight for the human rights I believe we all deserve in this country,' she continued. 'I believe in the fight for LGBTQ rights, and that any form of discrimination based on sexual orientation or gender is wrong. I believe that the systemic racism we still see in this country towards people of colour is terrifying, sickening and prevalent.'

Taylor Swift attends the InStyle and Warner Bros. Golden Globes After Party 2019 at the Beverly Hilton Hotel

In a 2019 interview with *Vanity Fair* magazine, Taylor went further in explaining her new-found enthusiasm for rolling her sleeves up and jumping into political debate. 'The Trump presidency forced me to lean in and educate myself. I found myself talking about government and the presidency and policy with my [then] boyfriend [actor Joe Alwyn], who supported me in speaking out,' she said.

'I started talking to my family and friends about politics and learning as much as I could about where I stand. I'm proud to have moved past fear and self-doubt, and to endorse and support leadership that moves us beyond this divisive, heart-breaking moment in time.'

Her seemingly effortless ability to command the millions of votes that candidates yearn for has since led political commentators to discuss very seriously whether she could actually swing the result of a presidential election. In the run up to the 2024 election, a source close to Republican nominee and former president Donald Trump told *Rolling Stone* magazine that his team would wage a 'holy war' on Taylor, if she endorsed his rival Joe Biden, as she had done in the 2020 election.

That same year Taylor might have begun to wish she had stayed out of politics, when conspiracy theorists began spreading the idea that she was a 'Psy-Op' (psychological operation) used by the Biden administration, or the Pentagon or the CIA – take your pick - to secretly influence public opinion and steer the result their way. While it's true that her reach and popularity is something that most politicians can only dream of, she does have rather a lot of other things to do at the moment!

In addition to her work as an activist, Taylor is renowned for her philanthropic efforts. Whether it's donating to disaster relief funds, supporting education initiatives, or aiding individuals in need, she devotes boundless energy and generous amounts of money to charitable causes.

She believes that kindness, inclusivity, and compassion are values worth fighting for and consistently demonstrates her commitment to supporting communities in need during times of crisis, including using her platform and resources to make a positive impact on those affected by natural disasters. Some of the significant contributions she has made include:

Hurricane Harvey Relief: In 2017, Taylor made a substantial donation to support relief efforts in the aftermath of Hurricane Harvey, which devastated parts of Texas and Louisiana. Her contribution helped provide aid to those affected by the storm, including shelter, food, and medical assistance.

Tennessee Tornado Relief: Following the devastating tornadoes that struck Tennessee in 2020, Taylor donated to relief organisations to support affected communities in her home state including families who had lost their homes.

Australian Bushfire Relief: In early 2020, Taylor pledged cash to support relief efforts for the devastating bushfires that ravaged Australia. Her contribution aided firefighting efforts, supported wildlife rescue and rehabilitation, and provided assistance to communities affected by the fires.

With an unwavering determination to do things her way – whether that's controlling the rights to her music, supporting victims of sexual abuse or working to improve the position of women in the music industry more generally, Taylor won't hesitate to get involved these days.

Taylor Swift's cash support helped the firefighting efforts during the 2020 Australian bushfire

As Taylor marches triumphantly towards 20 years in the music business her achievements are monumental.

While simply dazzling as one of the best ever singers and songwriters in the history of modern music, she has led the way in showing the power and relevance of live music in a post-streaming world. Creatively she shines, while having built a billion-dollar-plus business empire. And just when you think her list of achievements might be long enough, you remember that she's also a producer, a director, and an actor. Oh and also a philanthropist, a courageous advocate for artists' rights, an ardent feminist and a friend to any group facing discrimination.

Throughout all of this she has maintained a genuine emotional connection with her fans and successfully navigated the often harsh spotlight of celebrity life where every aspect of her being, from her braids to her boyfriends, is under constant scrutiny.

Commentators have speculated that Taylor is so influential that she could one day successfully run for political office herself– she has 283 million followers (and counting) on Instagram alone. But her legions of fans hope beyond hope that she'll stay in the music business, soundtracking their lives as long as they live.

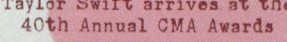

Taylor Swift arrives at the
40th Annual CMA Awards

Signs that she'll keep working were certainly looking good when Taylor released her 11th album *The Tortured Poets Department* on 19 April 2024. Taylor said that creating this album, about heartbreak and anguish, had reinforced her self-belief that songwriting is integral to her life. 'I have never had an album where I needed songwriting more than I needed it on Tortured Poets,' she said.

Although she concluded that 'This period of the author's life is now over, the chapter closed and boarded up,' the album's five star reviews and interesting collaborations with Post Malone and Florence Welch suggest she is far from finished with the music business.

And, as track 13, informs us she can even 'do it with a broken heart.'

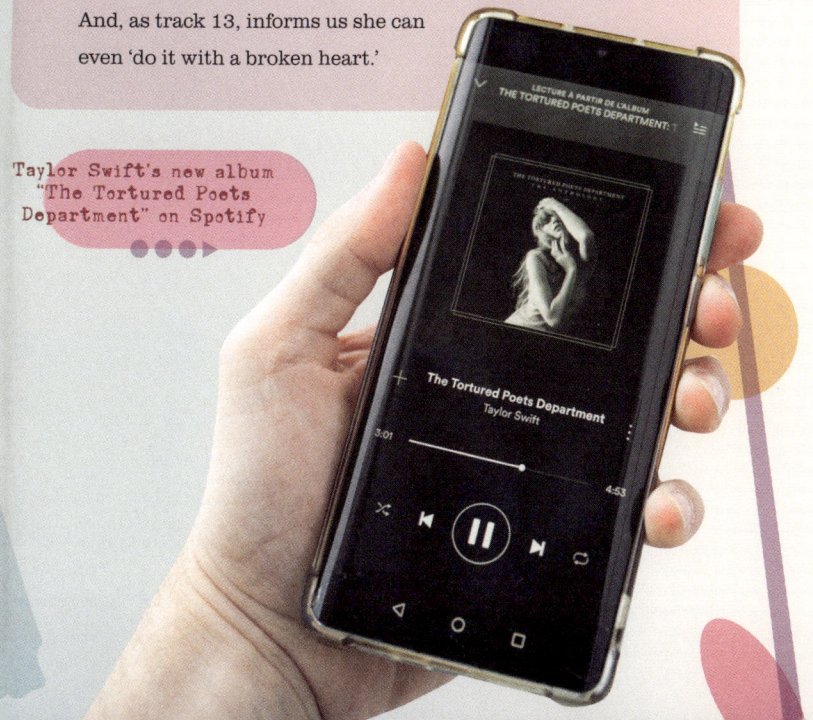

Taylor Swift's new album "The Tortured Poets Department" on Spotify